LONDON'S CHURCHES

LONDON'S CHURCHES

CHRISTOPHER HIBBERT
assisted by *Tessa Street*

with photographs by MARTIN BLACK

Macdonald
Queen Anne Press

A Queen Anne Press BOOK

© Christopher Hibbert 1988
Photographs copyright © Martin Black 1988

First published in Great Britain in 1988 by
Queen Anne Press, a division of
Macdonald & Co (Publishers) Ltd
3rd Floor
Greater London House
Hampstead Road
London
NW1 7QX

A Pergamon Press plc company

Bevis Marks photograph (page 24)
copyright © Spanish and Portuguese Jews' Congregation

Chapel Royal photographs (pages 83 and 85) reproduced by
gracious permission of Her Majesty the Queen

British Library Cataloguing in Publication Data

Hibbert, Christopher, 1924–
   London's churches.
   1. London. Church, to 1987. Architectural
   features
   I. Title
   726'.5'09421

ISBN 0–356–12762–1

Typeset by Butler & Tanner Ltd, Frome and London
Printed and bound in Hong Kong by Lee Fung Asco Printers

CONTENTS

INTRODUCTION

Towards the end of the sixth century, Ethelbert, King of Kent, rode from his capital to the coast to meet Augustine, the Prior of St Andrew's Monastery in Rome, who had been sent by the Pope to convert the heathen English to Christianity. Afraid of the stranger's magic, the King received him in the open air but, soon persuaded of his sincerity, he allowed him to preach to his people and within a few months became a Christian himself. Augustine was provided with a house for his followers in Canterbury, and in 597 was consecrated Bishop of the English. Seven years later another missionary from Rome, Mellitus, was established as Bishop in London where King Ethelbert built for him a church which was dedicated to St Paul. Mellitus, however, found the staunchly pagan Londoners far more intractable than Augustine had found the people of Kent and, after the death of his royal patron, the men of London drove their Bishop out of the city gates, returning to their old religion and their former priests. The see of London was then vacant for a number of years until a Northumbrian priest named Cedd, brother of St Chad, was appointed Bishop in 654.

By then a large number of churches had been built in the country, not only by the missionaries who had come to England from the Continent and their followers and converts, but also by missionaries from Scotland and Ireland. Most were constructed from split tree trunks, but some were made of stone, usually by foreign masons, and were designed in a simple Romanesque style with a nave and a semicircular apse, an architectural feature which did not appeal to English church builders of later periods. It was one of Cedd's successors as Bishop of London, Erconwald (c. 675– c.693), who founded a religious community at Barking in Essex for his sister, Ethelburga, and who endowed it with land on which was built the original church of ALL HALLOWS BY THE TOWER.

After the conquest by the Normans in 1066, numerous churches were built or rebuilt in what became known as an Anglo-Norman style. They had thick walls, often of rubble and mortar encased in stone, with nave and chancel and, usually, square east ends instead of the apses favoured in France. In London there remain from this time the CHAPEL OF ST JOHN IN THE TOWER, the crypts of ST MARY-LE-BOW and ST JOHN'S, CLERKENWELL, parts of ST BARTHOLOMEW THE GREAT, West Smithfield, and fragments of ST MARY MAGDALENE, Bermondsey.

RIGHT St Bartholomew the Great

BELOW Chapel of St John in the White Tower

Some Norman churches had sanctuaries as well as chancels; some were cruciform and several had towers, but most towers were added later, as were aisles. Windows had semicircular arches; but, soon after the middle of the twelfth century, the stronger pointed arch became more common, and with the appearance of the pointed arch there began to be developed those styles of architecture which later generations were first to condemn and later to praise as Gothic. The word Gothic as applied pejoratively to a supposedly barbarous architectural style did not come into use until the seventeenth century, and it was not until the early nineteenth century that Thomas Rickman, a Quaker doctor turned architect and author of *An Attempt to Discriminate the Styles of English Architecture*, first divided the style into three periods which, following a period of Transition, are still known as Early English (approximately corresponding with the thirteenth century), Decorated (fourteenth century), and Perpendicular (fifteenth century).

The Early English style is characterised by high and narrow lancet windows terminating in a pointed arch, by circular, or occasionally octagonal, pillars and by moulded capitals, sometimes carved with foliage. Most churches built in this period were provided with porches, and with towers or spires. Churches in the Decorated style differed little in plan but they tended to be larger, with wider aisles, bigger chancels, more altars for the celebration of Mass by the church's several priests, and with naves spacious enough to serve the purpose of general meeting places for the parishioners who strolled about on the rush-covered floor during the service, murmuring greetings, whispering to each other, sharing jokes with friends, and on occasions, according to one contemporary observer, 'chattering, laughing, jangling and jesting aloud' to such an extent that the priest 'smote his hand on the book to make them hold their peace; but there were some that would not'. On the walls all around them were paintings and, above them, the lancet windows which let in little light had been replaced by wider, more elaborate windows, divided by the intersecting stone ribwork called tracery.

The Black Death of 1348–9 interrupted church building for a time, but by the end of the fourteenth century the so-called Perpendicular Gothic style had been established in London, largely by the royal master masons who had worked at Westminster and Old St Paul's Cathedral. Walls

were now less thick, and windows larger and more numerous; porches were designed for the performance of the first part of baptisms and marriage services, and these porches frequently had upper chambers used for storage, schoolrooms or priests' dormitories. Towers were more imposing, and roofs were panelled and brightly painted. Indeed, colour was now splashed everywhere even more extravagantly than in the past. The pillars were decorated with geometrical lines, the walls were painted with scenes from the lives of saints or with such admonitory subjects as 'Judgement Day' and 'Souls in Torment'. The windows were filled with coloured glass. The rood, the figure of Christ on the Cross above the screen at the east end of the nave, was also coloured and often inappropriately clothed in garments of the gayest hue which were changed in accordance with the church's year. Candles were yellow, green, blue and red as well as white. Even the font was coloured and provided with a cover secured by a lock, since the water, changed only twice a year, would otherwise have been removed as a known cure for toothache, barrenness, impotence, fever and other complaints

ABOVE St Dunstan's and All Saints, Stepney

LEFT St Katharine Cree

and inadequacies. The pulpit, too, would have been painted if there were a pulpit at all. Pulpits were far from universal then: there are no pulpits at all in London churches of a date earlier than the middle of the fourteenth century.

According to Thomas Becket's secretary, William FitzStephen, there were already 126 parish churches in London at the end of the twelfth century when the population was about 20,000 to 25,000, as well as numerous chapels attached to monasteries and convents. And the number of both churches and chapels was constantly growing. The Augustinians built priories at St Mary Overie (St Mary over the river), traces of which survive in Southwark Cathedral, at Holy Trinity within Aldgate (*see* ST KATHARINE CREE) and at St Bartholomew West Smithfield (*see* ST BARTHOLOMEW THE LESS). Soon after the consecration of the Knights Hospitallers' priory

church of St John's, Clerkenwell, the Knights Templars built their round church known as the New Temple (*see* TEMPLE CHURCH); and, some years later, the Cistercians founded St Mary Graces in East Smithfield of which nothing survives. The great Cluniac priory of St Saviour's, Bermondsey, founded in 1084, was enlarged; so were the Carthusian foundation of Charterhouse, the Benedictine abbey at Westminster – for the lay inhabitants of whose precincts, ST MARGARET'S was built towards the middle of the twelfth century – and the Benedictine nunnery of St Helen's (*see* ST HELEN'S, BISHOPSGATE).

The coming of the friars from the Continent in the thirteenth century as missionaries to preach and minister to the poor – the Black Friars in 1221, the Grey Friars in 1223, the White Friars in 1241, the Austin Friars in 1253 and the Crossed or Crutched Friars in 1298 – increased the number of religious houses throughout the city, particularly in the poorer districts where the early friars first settled and where their selfless work amongst the sick and needy aroused the sympathy of the rich. Thus the Grey Friars, whose first small house was built in Stinking Lane near Newgate close by the butchers' shambles, earned the admiration of patrons with money to pay for the church, chapter house, priory and other buildings which eventually sprawled across many acres of ground between Newgate Street and St Bartholomew's Hospital, a hospital already a hundred years old when the Grey Friars came and still a hospital today. So, too, the Austin Friars, settling at first just inside the wall between Bishopsgate and Moorgate, were soon able to build themselves a church whose nave was even wider than that of Winchester Cathedral. At this time, also, the Black Friars – whose community was founded in Chancery Lane in 1221 – greatly extended their buildings when they were granted the two Norman riverside strongholds of Baynard's Castle and Montfichet Tower.

As well as the churches of the friaries, abbeys convents and nunneries there were, at the beginning of the fourteenth century, numerous small parish churches long since lost, built in odd corners of the city, above gateways and against what remained of the Roman wall. There were also chapels of ease offering services to parishioners for whom a walk to the parish church could not be lightly undertaken. ST MARY'S, STRATFORD LE BOW, for example, was a chapel of ease to ST DUNSTAN'S AND ALL SAINTS, STEPNEY. And, as well as chapels in palaces, such as the Chapels of St John and ST PETER AD VINCULA in the Tower, there were places where services were held and sermons delivered in the open air, as at Paul's Cross in the precincts of Old St Paul's Cathedral and the Spital Cross (see CHRIST CHURCH, SPITALFIELDS).

After the Dissolution of the Monasteries between 1536 and 1540 and the consequent destruction of many London churches, the population of the city, which may perhaps have been halved by the Black Death of 1348–49, began to increase rapidly and was probably about 200,000 by 1600 and 375,000 by 1650. Yet the religious and political troubles of these years, and the ending of benefactions by the suppression of chantries, inhibited the building of new churches. The churches that did appear were mostly in the late Gothic style until Inigo Jones, the King's Surveyor who had travelled in Italy where he had conceived a lasting admiration for the style associated with the name of the brilliant architect Andrea Palladio, began to design buildings in the classical manner. Jones's Banqueting House, the only remaining part of Whitehall Palace above ground, which was used for a time as a royal chapel, was completed in 1622; his QUEEN'S CHAPEL, MARLBOROUGH ROAD, designed for the Infanta of Spain, Charles I's intended bride, was begun in 1623 and, when finished in 1627, was the first Classical church in England; and his ST PAUL'S, COVENT GARDEN, a Tuscan pastiche, at once plain and majestic, was consecrated in 1638. ST KATHARINE CREE, rebuilt in 1628–30, has also been ascribed to Inigo Jones but the design is, in fact, by another hand. Jones did, however, work on Old St Paul's Cathedral which, when the Civil War broke out in 1642, 'contracted the Envy of all Christendom,' according to Jones's pupil, John Webb, 'for a Piece of Architecture not to be paralleled in these last ages of the World'.

By the end of the Civil War, during which the nave was used by the Parliamentarians as a cavalry barracks and the porch was let to seamstresses and pedlars, St Paul's had fallen into decay. And in 1663 the Dean and Chapter called upon Christopher Wren to suggest how best to carry out the necessary repairs. Wren, then aged thirty-one and recently appointed Professor of Astronomy at Oxford, where he had already designed the Sheldonian Theatre, strongly recommended demolition and reconstruction. The Dean and Chapter, refusing to consider this, continued to insist upon repair; and one of Wren's plans for this was accepted six days before the Great Fire of 1666 reduced the Cathedral to a shell.

Not only was Old St Paul's destroyed in the Great Fire; so were no less than eighty-eight parish churches. This, however, provided Wren with a great opportunity: fifty-one churches in the City were built or rebuilt under his direction, many of them on the awkwardly shaped sites upon which their predecessors had stood. They were paid for by a tax on coal as well as by parochial subscriptions, the woodwork, ironwork and furnishings being carried out by local craftsmen commissioned by the parishioners. With his great dome for St Paul's in mind, Wren imagined a dramatic accompanying skyline of towers, spires and steeples in white Portland stone or lead. Inside all of Wren's churches, the pulpit in the nave, the font at the west end, and the altar with its carved and sometimes painted altar-piece, were common and prominent features. All were lit by clear glass windows. But no two were quite the same: some were cruciform with a dome at the centre of the cross; some polygonal; others had only one aisle; yet others no aisle at all; a few were reconstructed with nave, aisles and rood screen in the manner of the Middle Ages. One, ST JAMES'S, PICCADILLY, was built outside the City on a virgin site to serve a newly developed, fashionable area.

The completion of several of Wren's churches was left to his surveyors, clerks and assistants. One of these assistants was Nicholas Hawksmoor who, recommended for his 'early skill and genius' for architecture, was taken on by Wren at the age of eighteen in 1679. Some years after this appointment, in 1710, the year in which St Paul's Cathedral was at last finished, a general election swept to power a High Church Tory government which celebrated its victory by bringing in an Act of Parliament for the building of fifty new churches 'in or near the Cities of London and Westminster or the suburbs thereof ... churches of stone and other proper Materials with Towers or Steeples to each of them'. These churches, it was vainly hoped, would bring the word of God to parts of London where lawbreakers abounded and would consequently induce a significant diminution in crime. Although the number so confidently inserted into the Act proved far too ambitious, a dozen fine new churches were built as a result of it, six of them

RIGHT Christ Church, Spitalfields

by Hawksmoor who had by now risen to fame as Sir Christopher Wren's most gifted and original pupil. So close, indeed, was Hawksmoor's association with Wren's later work that much of it seems to be imbued with the spirit of the younger man's genius, just as much of Hawksmoor's own work was inspired by the dramatic verve of John Vanbrugh, his near contemporary and, after 1699, his intimate collaborator. Three of Hawksmoor's six beautiful churches, all displaying a thrilling fusion of sombrely classical grandeur and Gothic or Baroque fancy, are in Tower Hamlets: ST GEORGE-IN-THE-EAST, CHRIST CHURCH, SPITALFIELDS, and ST ANNE'S, LIMEHOUSE. One is in Greenwich, ST ALFEGE; one in Camden, ST GEORGE'S, BLOOMSBURY; and the sixth, ST MARY WOOLNOTH is in the heart of the City, just east of the Mansion House.

Hawksmoor's colleague as Surveyor under the Act was William Dickinson, also a pupil of Wren, but none of the new churches was built to his designs and he resigned in 1713 to be replaced by the Scot James Gibbs who, dismissed as a Roman Catholic, was in turn succeeded by John James, a clergyman's son who was given the task of building ST GEORGE'S, HANOVER SQUARE, a church whose imposing columned portico was much admired and widely imitated.

Before his dismissal, however, Gibbs designed one of the most distinctive monuments of the London scene, the serenely dignified ST MARY-LE-STRAND, which so vividly displays in its Baroque overtones the architect's admiration for the contemporary architecture of Rome where he had at first studied for the priesthood. Gibbs's other great church in London, ST MARTIN-IN-THE-FIELDS, which was not one of the fifty churches, was more restrained, far more in tune, despite its tall, elaborate steeple, with the spirit of academic Palladianism. Finished in 1726, St Martin-in-the-Fields was in sharp contrast to two churches, ST JOHN'S, SMITH SQUARE and ST PAUL'S, DEPTFORD, designed by the wealthy gentleman architect, Thomas Archer, an admirer, like Gibbs, of Italian architecture, yet one whose extreme devotion to Baroque led to designs far more fanciful and bold than Gibbs had attempted in the Strand. A safer and less flamboyant architect in contemporary eyes was Henry Flitcroft, the son of William III's gardener, a protégé of that arch-priest of Palladianism, Lord Burlington – he was known as 'Burlington Harry' – and the man chosen both

for the rebuilding of St Olave's, Tooley Street, Southwark which was demolished in 1928, and for ST GILES-IN-THE-FIELDS which was completed in 1734. Many of these new churches were decorated and furnished as brightly and gaily as befitted the mood of the Restoration, often with ornamental details whose Christian symbolism was difficult to appreciate. Some churches were equipped with dog kennels; services were frequently attended in a light-hearted manner, as the diaries of Samuel Pepys make clear, and congregations often assembled for fashionable rather than religious purposes. The pews of the CHAPEL ROYAL, ST JAMES'S PALACE actually had to be heightened to prevent ogling; and a female character in Vanbrugh's *The Relapse* (1696) asks Lord Foppington which church he most obliges with his presence:

Lord Foppington: *Oh! St James's, madam: there's much the best company.*
Amanda: *Is there good preaching too?*
Lord Foppington: *Why, faith, madam, I can't tell. A man must have very little to do there that can give an account of the sermon.*

When there was good preaching, 'there pre-

vailed in those days,' according to Samuel Johnson, 'an indecent custom; when the preacher touched any favourite topic, in a manner that delighted his audiences, their approbation was expressed by a loud hum, continued in proportion to their zeal and pleasure. When Burnet preached, part of his congregation hummed so loudly that he sat down to enjoy it, and rubbed his face in his handkerchief.'

After the last of the churches built under the 1711 Act had been completed, the building of new churches was left to the enterprise of individual parishes or to the generosity of individuals. Baroque was not to the taste of the new builders who preferred the Palladian style and who much admired St Martin-in-the-Fields whose architect obligingly produced a book containing drawings of the building for the guidance of those who wanted a church like it. Several such churches were built with interiors closely resembling St Martin's, such as ST PETER'S, VERE STREET which was opened at Easter 1724 to serve the residents of the new

LEFT St Anne's, Limehouse

BELOW Chapel Royal, St James's Palace

estate which the Earl of Oxford was developing around Cavendish Square.

The interiors of churches were, indeed, considered at this time quite as important as their exteriors. All rate-payers in the parish were entitled to have their own pews; and they liked these pews to be substantial box pews, well made and nicely carved. If there was insufficient room on the ground floor, galleries would be built along the southern and northern walls, as extensions of the western gallery where the choir sang and the organ was played. The floor of the nave was usually paved in stone, the sanctuary often in squares of black and white marble. The roof was generally ceiled; the pulpit still prominent; the altar enclosed by rails. Interiors altered a little when, towards the end of the century, architects and their patrons tended to grow tired of the rather heavily pretentious forms into which neo-Palladianism had fallen and when Robert Adam and his brothers and successors, notably James Wyatt, set out to provide them with something more delicate.

Many churchmen, however, considered the style associated with the brothers Adam wholly unsuited to a building dedicated to God. Many others were as ready to condemn the influence of the Grecian world which was to inspire ST PANCRAS NEW CHURCH, ALL SAINTS, CAMDEN STREET and ST PETER'S, EATON SQUARE. To such men it seemed high time to return to the Gothic.

◆

Little church building was carried out in the twenty-five years of intermittent warfare which was ended by the Battle of Waterloo, but in 1818 the Church Building Society was founded and under the Church Building Act of the same year, Parliament empowered Commissioners to spend £1,000,000 (later increased to £1,500,000) on the construction of churches as a thanksgiving – so some supporters of the Act maintained – for Britain's victory over Napoleon. The Commissioners' London Churches, known popularly as Waterloo Churches, were mostly either Greek or Gothic, and many of them were made larger than the money available for them would reasonably allow, to cater for a population which had increased from 650,000 in 1750 to 1,139,355 in 1811. In all thirty-eight new churches were built in London during the ten years after 1818, and while several were undistinguished, there were some of high quality,

ABOVE St Pancras New Church

LEFT St Peter's, Walworth

among them ST PETER'S, WALWORTH, HOLY TRINITY, MARYLEBONE and ST JOHN ON BETHNAL GREEN, all by Sir John Soane. Other interesting churches were constructed independently of the Commissioners at this time, such as Thomas Hardwick's ST MARYLEBONE PARISH CHURCH with its magnificent hexastyle Corinthian portico, and ALL SOULS, LANGHAM PLACE designed as part of his scheme for Regent Street and Regent's Park by John Nash who dismayed contemporary taste by his combination of a Greek peristyle with a spire.

This unorthodoxy seemed particularly shocking at a time when the virtues of pure Gothic were being more widely recognised. Rickman's celebrated book had appeared in 1817 and was constantly reprinted, and Augustus Welby Pugin's influential and provocative *Contrasts* was first published in 1836. It was Pugin's contention that Gothic was the one and only suitable style for Christian architecture, and those students of church building and decoration known as ecclesiologists who agreed with him maintained that the stone of which a church was built must be real not artificial, that the architect should be a Christian, and that the interior of a church should be properly arranged. They also maintained that the choir must be in the chancel, not in a gallery at the west end; that the ostentatious three-decker pulpit must be replaced by a pulpit of more modest construction, and high, box pews by low open ones; that dormer windows in the roof and plaster ceilings must be removed together with galleries; that the lessons should be read from a lectern; and that the font should invariably be at the west end. Gradually the didactic rules of the ecclesiologists became almost universally accepted, and during the great age of church restoration which began in the 1840s they were generally observed without question, often destroying the charm of a church which, while no doubt in need of repair, could well have done without such drastic reconstruction.

While old churches were being restored, new ones were being built, many of them with the help of the Metropolis New Churches Fund established by Charles James Blomfield, the Bishop of London, who in 1834 had drawn attention to ten parishes in his diocese with a population of well over 350,000. In these parishes there were, he said, no more than eighteen churches and chapels served by twenty-four incumbents and curates, that was to say less than one church or chapel for every 19,000 people, and one clergyman for every 14,000. It was, Blomfield insisted, 'a work of prudence no less than charity' to provide these people with more churches and to 'reclaim hundreds of thousands of the poor from practical heathenism'. Although disappointed by the result of his appeal for funds, seventy-eight new churches were wholly or partly built by Blomfield's Fund, and when he resigned in 1856 he had consecrated almost two hundred churches in his diocese, including Thomas Cundy's Gothic ST BARNABAS, PIMLICO.

Blomfield was succeeded by Archibald Campbell Tait, born a Presbyterian and later Archbishop of Canterbury, who in 1863 proposed the establishment of a Bishop of London's Fund of £500,000 (later increased to £1 million) to which he himself contributed £2,000 and to which Queen Victoria gave £3,000. Like Blomfield, Tait was disappointed by the initial response to his appeal, but eventually the Fund was able to contribute to the construction of forty-one more churches.

The names of the celebrated Victorian architects responsible for these churches, and for others built by local church building associations, appear frequently in the following pages. William Butterfield, architect of Keble College, Oxford, was responsible for ST ALBAN THE MARTYR, HOLBORN and ALL SAINTS, MARGARET STREET, intended as the Ecclesiological Society's model church; J. L. Pearson designed ST AUGUSTINE'S, KILBURN and ST JOHN'S, UPPER NORWOOD as well as ST PETER'S, VAUXHALL, described by Sir John Betjeman as 'exactly what a Victorian High church in a poor district ought to be'; Sir George Gilbert Scott, the self-styled interpreter of the Gothic Revival for the uninitiated, who is believed to have built or restored over seven hundred churches, designed ST MARY ABBOTS, KENSINGTON CHURCH STREET, and Sir Arthur Blomfield, son of the Bishop, built ALL SAINTS, FULHAM. J. F. Bentley, architect of Westminster Cathedral, was responsible for the Convent of the SACRED HEART, HAMMERSMITH ROAD and the interior of the CHURCH OF THE ASSUMPTION, WARWICK STREET, G. E. Street for ST, JAMES THE LESS, THORNDIKE STREET, ST JAMES'S, SUSSEX GARDENS and ST MARY MAGDALENE, PADDINGTON, and S. S. Teulon for transforming ST GEORGE THE MARTYR, QUEEN SQUARE.

As new churches, often now of brick, appeared for the benefit of the populations of the suburbs brought into existence by the coming of the railways, so others were demolished to make way for the iron rails and the station platforms, the shunting yards, repair shops and coal bunkers, as well as for new developments of office blocks, shops and housing. In the City alone, twenty churches were lost between 1841 and 1908, some of them works of outstanding merit such as Wren's St Antholin's, Budge Row, demolished in 1874. The bombs of the Second World War destroyed many more churches in London. Some of these had been built in the 1920s and 1930s, when many new churches appeared, though none of any great distinction. Far more regrettable was the loss of older churches, among them Wren's St Alban's, Wood Street which was gutted in 1940, and, another Wren church, St Mildred's, Bread Street, destroyed in 1941. Few London churches built since then are worthy of special remark.

◆

RIGHT St Mary Abbots

Well over three hundred churches are provided with separate entries in *The London Encyclopaedia* (ed. Ben Weinreb and Christopher Hibbert, 1983). I have had to content myself with less than half that number; and my choice is necessarily subjective and arbitrary. I have for the most part limited myself to churches in the City and Westminster and in the inner boroughs which are within a few miles of St Paul's Cathedral. I am most grateful to the incumbents, too numerous to mention here, who have answered my questions and those of Tessa Street; to Dawn Marriott who has provided us with material on several of the North London churches; to Matthew Ryan for his great assistance with the churches in East London; to Margaret Lewendon who has typed the manuscript; and to my wife who has made the index. A brief bibliography is given at the end of the book but, in addition to acknowledging the use I have made of the guides and histories available in many of the churches, I should like to express here my gratitude to those whose works I have found particularly helpful, to Mervyn Blatch, to Basil F. L. Clarke, to the late Sir Nikolaus Pevsner, the late Sir John Betjeman, and Elizabeth and Wayland Young. Finally, I am extremely grateful to Donald Findlay of the Council for the Care of Churches for having read the typescript with such care.

In addition, Martin Black would like to thank the following for their kind co-operation in the taking of photographs: Nutt and Oliver solicitors, the Lord Chamberlain's office, Brigadier Kenneth Mears, Rev. Chris Idle, Mr Fred Battes, Mr Alan Lennox, Sue of TA London, Mr Ken Allen, Rev. Edward Thompson, Robert Heron of Anniversary Press, Mr Trimmer, Father Richard Price, Rev. Dr R. Gibbins, the Masters of the Bench of the Inner Temple, all at St Paul's Hammersmith, John Davies of Lloyds Insurance, Mr Duce of Sun Life, Alan Rusby, Rev. Peter Harding, Father Raymond Olivier Jovenez, the Commander of the College and the Trustee of the Greenwich Hospital and A. G. Penman, Assistant Civil Secretary RNC. Thanks also to countless others who unlocked churches, moved cars, turned on floodlights and granted access to vantage points across the capital.

Editor's note: Churches in this book have been grouped according to London boroughs. For easy reference, a postcode index can be found on page 221.

◆

CITY OF LONDON

◆

ALL HALLOWS BY THE TOWER
Byward Street, EC3

All Hallows stands by itself on a prominent site adjacent to the Tower of London. The church of St Dunstan was irretrievably damaged during the Second World War and its parish is now joined to All Hallows. Originally known as 'All Hallows Berkyngechirche by the Tower', it was then attached to the Abbey of Barking (Berkynge), which had been founded by Erconwald, Bishop of London, in about 675. The foundation of the church dates from about the same period, the Saxon remains which have been uncovered suggesting that it measured approximately 24 feet by 70 feet and was without aisles. It was probably succeeded by a Norman church, built about ten years after the Tower of London, and this seems to have been enlarged in the late twelfth century. In the fourteenth century the chancel was renewed and a crypt, with a ribbed barrel vault, was built below the south chancel aisle. Earlier, in the mid-thirteenth century, a Lady Chapel, alleged to have been founded by Richard Cœur de Lion, was built in the churchyard to the north. Under Edward IV this chapel became a royal chantry, but in spite of its illustrious associations it was completely demolished in 1547 after the Reformation and no trace of it remains. In 1649 the medieval church

tower was weakened by a nearby explosion and was replaced in 1658–9 by a plain red brick tower which is set at an angle to the axis of the church and flanked by a charming vestry completed in 1932. After the Great Fire of 1666 in which All Hallows narrowly escaped destruction, Samuel Pepys mounted the new tower from which he saw 'the saddest sight of desolation'.

The church was severely damaged during the bombing of 1940. Much of the walling survived, however, as did the aisles with some fifteenth-century windows above, the crypt, the two-storey porch of the 1880s, the undercroft of 1925, the vestry and the tower. When it was rebuilt in 1948–57 by Seely and Paget no attempt was made to reconstruct the old church. Nonetheless its style is basically Perpendicular with pillars of Painswick limestone. It was rededicated in 1957, and a slender classical spire of Columbian pine, sheathed in copper, now adorns the tower.

Little is left of its medieval atmosphere, but there are some Saxon remains incorporated in the building, including part of the east wall to the crypt and an arch of Roman brick on the south

RIGHT Font cover by Grinling Gibbons,
All Hallows by the Tower

BELOW All Hallows by the Tower

side. The undercroft below the nave houses a Roman tessellated pavement and a collection of Roman relics, together with fragments of three Saxon crosses which were uncovered at various times after the bombing.

Resting upon a new font made of Gibraltar limestone by a Sicilian prisoner-of-war is an exquisite font cover carved by Grinling Gibbons, which is among the few furnishings to have survived the war. Others are the Wren pulpit, taken from St Swithun's, London Stone, which was destroyed by bombing in 1941, and the rails of the lectern which date from 1613. The four panels used as an altarpiece in the north aisle are unique survivals from the chantry chapel. The organ is post-war and was built in 1957 by Harrison and Harrison (in a case based on Renatus Harris's destroyed case of 1675), and there is a modern mural of the Last Supper by Brian Thomas behind the altar table.

All Hallows by the Tower is the parish church of H. M. Customs and Excise and the London World Trade Centre. It is also a brass rubbing centre.

ABOVE All Hallows London Wall

LEFT Bevis Marks Synagogue

ALL HALLOWS LONDON WALL
London Wall, at Broad Street, EC2
(George Dance the Younger, 1765-7)

All Hallows stands on a long narrow fringe of land which once flanked the old boundary of London, hence its dedication. The vestry is actually built upon a bastion of the underlying old Roman wall and follows its semi-circular shape. Of the two earlier churches which stood on the site, the first is thought to have been built in or before the reign of Henry I; the second, which also served the former parish of St Augustine on the Wall, dated from the thirteenth century. A modest, low structure with a weatherboarded tower and Perpendicular windows, it survived the Great Fire but fell into decay in the eighteenth century. The present church was designed by George Dance the Younger who was only twenty-four at the time. It was constructed at a cost of about £3,000 and was completed in 1767. The interior was refurnished in 1891 by Sir Arthur Blomfield. After severe bomb damage in 1941 it was left derelict for twenty years, but was finally restored with great sensitivity by David Nye and reconsecrated in 1962. It is now a Guild Church, the headquarters of the Council for the Care of Churches and the parish has been united with that of St Botolph's, Bishopsgate.

Its plain brick exterior with its high semi-circular windows, low west tower with stone cupola and rounded eastern apse, in no way prepares the visitor for the elegance within. George Dance's interior, remarkable in its time for its sparingness of detail and delicacy of design, gives an effect of light and grace. There are fine plaster motifs on the tunnel-vault of the nave, which is carried by fluted Ionic columns, and a charming pattern of lozenges and rosettes over the apse. The church is without aisles. Over the altar hangs a painting by Sir Nathaniel Dance-Holland, given by his brother the architect. The small nineteenth-century organ was built in about 1880 for a private house in Islington and came to All Hallows' from Islington Parish Hall in 1960. The font is from St Mary Magdalene, Old Fish Street, and there is a fine chandelier of 1766, one of a pair made by Lukyn Betts, a parishioner who afterwards went bankrupt. The pulpit is unusual in that it can only be approached through the vestry.

An interesting feature of the churchyard is the section of London wall which forms its northern boundary.

BEVIS MARKS SYNAGOGUE
Heneage Lane, off Bevis Marks, EC3
(Joseph Avis, 1700-01)

Bevis Marks is a corruption of Burics Marks, the town house of the Abbot of Bury St Edmunds which once stood here. The synagogue was erected for the Jewish community which had grown up in the City during the seventeenth century. It was built by Joseph Avis, a carpenter by trade, a Quaker by religion, who reputedly returned most of his fee to the congregation, being reluctant to make a profit from building a sacred house. It is of brick, plain and unassuming on the outside, with a charming west front facing onto a courtyard. The interior, similar in character to a contemporary nonconformist chapel, has three galleries supported on wooden Tuscan pillars and a flat ceiling; the domestic-looking seats face inwards towards each other. The general impression is one of beauty and serenity; the rich furnishings are carved by the same skilled craftsmen who made the fittings for the neighbouring City churches of the same period. The light shining in from the large, clear glass windows is reflected in the gleaming, curling arms of the gorgeous brass chandeliers, seven in number, one of which came from a sister synagogue, opened in 1675 in Amsterdam.

Bevis Marks, the oldest Jewish synagogue in this

ABOVE Church of the Holy Sepulchre

RIGHT St Andrew Undershaft

country, is unique for its preservation and still traditional in its services, to which Christians are welcome.

CHURCH OF THE HOLY SEPULCHRE
WITHOUT NEWGATE Holborn Viaduct, EC1

Originally dedicated to St Edmund, this church assumed its present name during the Crusades. First mentioned in 1137, it was rebuilt in the mid-fifteenth century by Sir John Popham, Treasurer to Henry VI. Further rebuilding took place between 1624 and 1634. Shortly before this, in compliance with the terms of a legacy from a parishioner, a gruesome custom had arisen. On the eve of an execution, the sexton would walk along an underground passage linking the church to Newgate Gaol ringing his handbell outside the condemned cell and intoning these words:

> *Examine well yourselves. In time repent*
> *That you may not to eternal flames be sent.*
> *And when St Sepulchre's bell tomorrow tolls*
> *The Lord have mercy on your souls.*

Following this awesome admonition, the victim would be offered a nosegay as he passed the church gate in the morning. This practice ceased only in 1744, and the handbell is still displayed in the church.

St Sepulchre's was gutted in the Great Fire, and the parishioners, reluctant to wait for Christopher Wren, seemingly caused offence by employing his master mason, Joshua Marshall, to rebuild their church. It was reopened in 1670. Since then the outside has been altered twice to suit the fluctuations of fashion and the fabric has been so extensively renewed that, today, the only authentic fifteenth-century features are the fan vault of the porch and the (restored) arches under the tower. The outside is Victorian Perpendicular with the walls refaced in Portland stone. The fifteenth-century tower, restored in 1711–14 and again in 1878 when it was given its top-heavy pinnacles, is in ragstone.

Inside, a miscellany of architectural styles reflects the various restorations. The Musicians' Chapel to the north, formerly dedicated to St Stephen, contains some fifteenth-century work. It also houses the ashes of Sir Henry Wood, who was christened here in 1870 and, as a boy, learned to play the organ in this church. On the south side is the Regimental Chapel of the Royal Fusiliers. Some of the furnishings date from the post-Fire restoration. These include two fine fonts, one of which came from Christchurch, Newgate, and the case of a Renatus Harris organ of 1677, rebuilt in 1932 by Arthur Harrison.

The first Smithfield martyr, John Rogers, was Rector here from 1550 until his death in 1555. Roger Ascham, tutor to Queen Elizabeth and Lady Jane Grey, was buried here in 1568, and there is a memorial to the adventurous Captain John Smith, one-time Governor of Virginia, who died in 1631.

Today St Sepulchre's is the church of the Royal School of Church Music, and provides the setting for many musical events.

ST ANDREW UNDERSHAFT
Leadenhall Street, EC3 (1520-32)

A church has stood here since at least the twelfth century. The present church takes its name from a shaft or maypole which, from the fifteenth century, was set up each May Day beside the tower. According to John Stow, after the riot of City apprentices on Evil May Day, 1517, in which many people were killed, the maypole was repositioned under the eaves of a row of houses in what was later known as Shaft Alley; and there it remained until 1549 when the residents, incited by an inflammatory sermon against pagan practices, took it down, chopped it up and burned it.

When it was rebuilt in 1520–32, St Andrew Undershaft retained its fifteenth-century tower with its prominent newel stair turret. Repaired and renovated at various times during the subsequent three centuries, the church was again restored in 1930 when some of its period features, removed in earlier restorations, were replaced. In 1949–50, the almost flat, panelled roof was rebuilt and the original 125 carved and gilt bosses, each one different, were put back. St Andrew's is one of only four City churches to have escaped intact both the Great Fire and the bombing of the Second World War; but in 1976, it was slightly damaged by fire. It has since been restored, and its lofty light interior is in keeping with its plain sixteenth-century exterior.

There are some fine seventeenth-century furnishings, including a plain marble octagonal font of 1631 and a notable organ in a Renatus Harris case of 1696. The Tijou communion rails of 1704, removed by Sir Arthur Blomfield during his restoration of 1875–6, were reinstated in 1930. Among the many monuments is one to the London chronicler John Stow, who died in 1605 and whose church this was. He sits in marble effigy at his writing table, and each year at a memorial service, the Lord Mayor puts a new quill pen into his hand and presents the old one, together with a copy of Stow's *Survey of London*, to the child who has written the best essay on London. Another monument is to Samuel Pepys' childless uncle, William Wight, who proposed to Mrs Pepys that he and she should have a child between them so that he could make it his heir. Pepys commented in his Diary, 'I fear all his kindness is but his lust for her.'

All that is left of the churchyard is a very small garden on the north side. The church, which is run by the staff of St Helen's, Bishopsgate, is used for concerts, talks and discussion groups as well as for its traditional functions.

ST BARTHOLOMEW-THE-GREAT
West Smithfield, at Cloth Fair, EC1

Early in the twelfth century, Rahere, a former jester at Henry I's court, having undergone a religious conversion, visited Rome on a pilgrimage. Here he fell ill with malaria and, in gratitude for his recovery, on his return founded a hospital 'for the restoration of poor men'. At the same time, prompted by a vision of St Bartholomew, he also established an Augustinian priory upon an adjoining site in Smithfield, which he dedicated to the saint and of which he became the first prior. It seems likely that the eastern parts of the priory church, including the choir, ambulatory and a Lady Chapel, were completed and consecrated in 1123. To these were later added the transepts and a great nave and, in about 1405, the church was further extended by the addition of a new Lady Chapel. There were further additions and alterations early in the fifteenth century, and in about

RIGHT St Bartholomew-the-Less

BELOW St Bartholomew-the-Great

1515 a very pretty oriel window was constructed on the south side of the chancel by William Bolton, prior from 1500 to 1532, to serve as a private chapel accessible from his lodgings.

The hospital was separated from the priory in 1420 after continual disputes about tithes and such matters as who should have the bigger bells and who should ring them first. The present St Bartholomew's Hospital stands upon its site.

At the Dissolution of the Monasteries the priory was surrendered to the king who sold it to Sir Richard Rich, the chancel being retained for parish worship; but a large part of the church, including the nave, was either demolished or fell into ruin, and the priory buildings were sold for lay use. The subsequent dilapidation was such that, in 1563, Bishop Grindal pressed for the conversion of the refectory into a place of worship: 'I assure you, without partialitie, if it were roofed up, it were farre more beautiful and conveniente than the other.' This suggestion was not taken up, however, and in 1622-8 the church was repaired, a brick tower, 'very richly and fairly finished', being built at the curtailed west end to replace the earlier central tower.

Thereafter St Bartholomew's suffered progressive deterioration and such unseemly encroachments as a blacksmith's forge in the north transept, a carpenter's shop and hop store in the sacristy, stables in the cloisters and a fringe-making works in the Lady Chapel, until, in the nineteenth century, there were a number of repairs and renovations and most of the secular activities were banished. A major restoration, begun in 1884, was carried out with great care by Sir Aston Webb who succeeded in removing even the obdurate fringe-factory and returned the church to something of its former grandeur. Today, the interior is much darker than in late medieval times since the rebuilding of the truncated end of the church removed the big windows which had lightened it. Nevertheless, the effect is deeply impressive: the great stone choir with its massive pillars supporting plain round arches, together with the almost complete absence of decoration, presents a magnificent example of Norman architecture. The early rounded arches on the east and west sides of the crossing make an interesting contrast to the Gothic arches on the north and south sides.

Among the monuments which adorn the church there is one to Rahere, erected about 300 years after his death in 1143, which shows him lying on a tomb chest under a canopy. Most of the furnishings are of the nineteenth century, but there is an octagonal stone font of the fifteenth century in which William Hogarth was baptised in 1697.

The cloister, which was substantially rebuilt in the 1920s, now houses a museum. The outside has been refaced in flint and Portland stone.

◆

ST BARTHOLOMEW-THE-LESS
West Smithfield, EC1
(Thomas Hardwick, 1823-5)

First called 'The Chapel of the Holy Cross', St Bartholomew-the-Less was originally one of four chapels attached to the hospital founded by Henry I's former court jester, Rahere, in the early twelfth century. It stands to the left just inside the hospital precincts where there has been a church since about 1184. In 1547, at the Dissolution of the Monasteries, it was made the parish church for the refounded St Bartholomew's Hospital.

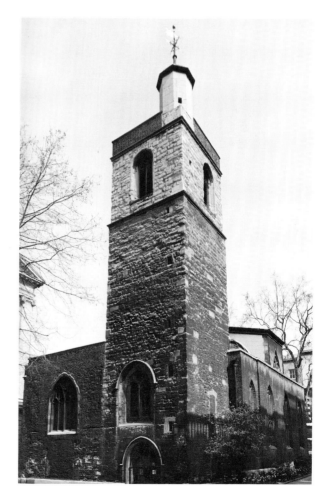

In 1789 it was rescued from a state of dilapidation by George Dance the Younger, whose unusual plan of an octagon framed by the existing church but extending beyond the east wall and above the roof, was constructed in wood. All too soon, however, the wooden structure was consumed by dry rot, and in 1823–5 it was replaced by one similar, but in stone and iron, designed by Thomas Hardwick. At the same time Hardwick rebuilt the crumbling medieval stone walls in brick. About forty years later his grandson, P. C. Hardwick, renovated the sanctuary and added some tracery to the upper windows.

Badly damaged during the Second World War, the odd but attractive little church was restored by Seely and Paget and reopened in 1951. There is no vestige of the Norman structure to be seen today, the earliest part being the plain stone tower which dates from the fifteenth century. The octagonal interior is modestly decorated in grey and white and the fittings are mainly Victorian. Among the monuments are a number commemorating past surgeons and physicians of the Hospital.

Inigo Jones was baptised here in 1573.

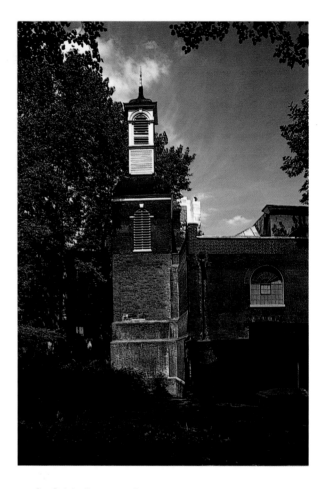

◆

ST BOTOLPH'S, ALDERSGATE
Aldersgate, EC1
(Nathaniel Wright, 1788-91)

This church is one of three now remaining which were built near the City gates for the benefit of travellers. The original eleventh-century foundation was replaced in the mid-fourteenth century by a traditional medieval church with nave and aisles. This survived into the eighteenth century, but by then it was so decayed that the parish petitioned repeatedly for a new church. Their prayers were finally granted and the rebuilding, under Nathaniel Wright, District Surveyor for the area, took place between 1788–91. In 1830–31 the east wall was set back to allow for improvements to the approach to the nearby General Post Office. It was rebuilt in stucco and contains a Venetian window between coupled Ionic columns. Otherwise, the exterior is of the plainest brick with

ABOVE RIGHT St Botolph's, Aldersgate

LEFT St Bartholomew-the-Great

arched windows and a west tower surmounted by a charming wooden cupola.

In complete contrast, the well-preserved eighteenth-century interior is extremely elegant with coffered apses at each end, the east one in blue and gold. The wooden galleries on the north and south sides rise on square piers, the west gallery curving forward and containing the organ. Below the galleries are fine plaster friezes. The beautiful blue ceiling is lit by high lunette windows and is decorated with large plaster rosettes. The furnishings include a late eighteenth-century pulpit of inlaid mahogany on a pedestal shaped like a palm, an organ by Samuel Green dating from 1778, and glass of 1788 in the east window depicting The Agony in the Garden. This is by James Pearson from designs by Nathaniel Clarkson.

A most attractive feature is the large garden to the south which, comprising several local churchyards, is known as Postman's Park from its proximity to the General Post Office. It contains a memorial cloister recording acts of heroism by men and women in everyday life. The earliest tablet commemorates 'Sarah Smith, Pantomime Artiste at Prince's Theatre, who died of horrible injuries received when attempting in her inflammable dress to extinguish the flames which had enveloped her companion. January 24th 1863.' On the south side is a powerful bronze statue of the Minotaur by Michael Ayrton. By the Aldersgate entrance to the garden is a plaque erected in 1926 to commemorate the conversion of Charles and John Wesley, the latter having felt his heart 'strangely warmed' on this spot.

In 1954 St Botolph's became a Guild Church.

ST BOTOLPH'S, ALDGATE
Aldgate, EC3
(George Dance the Elder, 1741-4)

Like St Botolph's, Aldersgate and St Botolph's Without Bishopsgate, this church was built near one of the main gates of the City to meet the spiritual needs of travellers and was dedicated to their patron saint. The first place of worship on the site was a Saxon foundation, mentioned early in the twelfth century when it was acquired by the Priory of Holy Trinity. Just before the Reformation it was rebuilt and enlarged since, according to John Stow, 'the parishioners of this parish being of late years mightily increased, the church is pestered with lofts and seats for them'. At the Dissolution of the Monasteries St Botolph's was annexed by the Crown.

By 1740 the Tudor structure had become decayed and George Dance the Elder was commissioned to design another. During the demolition of the medieval church the body of a boy was discovered upright in a vault, his intestines clearly visible. People paid 2d. to observe this gruesome sight. Dance's new church (which, unconventionally, faces north to south) was completed and consecrated in 1744. It is in red brick with Venetian windows on three sides. The south tower with its obelisk spire is flanked by domed side entrances. In 1889 the interior was altered by J. F. Bentley whose decorative treatment of the ceiling with its figured coving, while not in keeping with its eighteenth-century character, is undeniably original. Bentley also designed the reredos. After a fire in 1966 further restoration was carried out by Rodney Tatchell. This included the formation at the south end of an attractive octagonal baptistry which now houses the eighteenth-century circular font. The Renatus Harris organ was 'ye gift of Mr Thomas Whiting to the hole

St Botolph's, Aldgate

Parrish 1676'. There is a peal of eight bells cast by Lester and Pack in 1744. On the east wall is an exceptionally interesting seventeenth-century carved panel, in the manner of Grinling Gibbons, which came from St Mary Matfelon, Whitechapel Road (destroyed in the Second World War).

There are a number of literary associations attached to this church. Geoffrey Chaucer lived in the parish in 1374; Edmund Spenser was born here in the mid-sixteenth century; and Daniel Defoe was married here in 1683. In his account of the Great Plague he mentions the two great pits in St Botolph's churchyard which were filled, in four months, with over 5,000 victims. Among the intriguing monuments is one of 1715 to Benjamin Pratt who 'affected to end his days in celibacy'.

Today, St Botolph's is the headquarters of the Diocesan Council for Christian/Jewish understanding, and many of its parishioners are Jewish. Half the crypt contains a mission for the homeless. Exhibitions of art are now held in the church.

St Botolph's Without Bishopsgate

ST BOTOLPH'S WITHOUT BISHOPSGATE
Bishopsgate, EC2 (James Gould and George Dance the Elder, 1727-9)

First mentioned in about 1212, the original church was built just outside the City walls on the main road to the north, and like St Botolph's, Aldersgate and St Botolph's, Aldgate, it was dedicated to the patron saint of travellers. There is a reference in its early history to a female hermit who resided in the churchyard and was in receipt of 40s. a year from the Sheriff. John Stow, writing in the late sixteenth century, describes the said 'fair' churchyard as 'adjoining to the town ditch, upon the very bank thereof, but of old time inclosed with a comely wall of brick'.

The medieval building survived the Great Fire but afterwards fell into ruin and was replaced by a new church, designed by James Gould and his son-in-law, George Dance the Elder, which was consecrated in 1728. In 1828 an additional church,

All Saints, Skinner Street, was built to help accommodate the much increased population of the parish, but this was demolished in 1869. Towards the end of the nineteenth century St Botolph's was considered to be one of the richest livings in London. The Rev. William Rogers, who was the incumbent at this time, has left an entertaining account of his efforts to transform the decayed churchyard he found into a garden of recreation: 'The Rectory front door was besieged by heartbroken descendants', who feared violation to the bones of their ancestors. However, in the words of his churchwarden, 'a dozen of sherry at 30s. squared the lot of them', and his project was carried. Indeed, for a time the new garden even featured a sort of 'zoo', until 'the screams of the peacocks disturbed the devotions of the congregation'.

There have been a number of improvements and restorations to the church since it was built, notably the insertion of a glass dome in 1828, and the remodelling of the chancel fifty years later. The exterior is in plain red brick with two-tiered round-headed windows, and an east tower faced with stone. Inside, there are deep galleries on three sides beneath which are inscribed in gold the names of previous rectors in a line around the church, starting with John of Northampton and Henry of Colne, 1323. A coved ceiling resting on Corinthian columns is lit by the dome. The pulpit and lectern are contemporary with the church. Edward Alleyn, founder of Dulwich College, was baptised here in 1566 and John Keats in 1795.

To the west of the church stands the 1861 parish hall, restored in 1952 by the Worshipful Company of Fan Makers, on the front of which, in separate niches, stand the figures of two charity children in painted Coade stone brought here from the former school building in Peter Street.

◆

ST DUNSTAN'S IN THE WEST
Fleet Street, EC4 (John Shaw, 1829-33)

The dedication to the tenth-century saint suggests that there may have been a Saxon church on this site, since a Norman prohibition forbade new churches being named after Saxon saints. However, no trace of one remains, and the first mention of a place of worship here is in the twelfth century. In the thirteenth century it was known as St Dunstan's West to distinguish it from St

Dunstan in the East (destroyed in the Second World War) which stood near the Tower. Structurally it appears to have followed the medieval pattern of a nave, arcades and an arched roof.

During the sixteenth century, William Tyndale, translator of the New Testament, carried out duties as a curate here. In the following century, John Donne, poet and divine, was rector of the parish from 1624 until his death in 1631, although he complained he received no stipend. In 1667 Samuel Pepys recounts how he, 'being weary, turned into St Dunstan's Church, where I hear an able sermon ... and stood by a pretty, modest maid whom I did labour to take by the hand and body, but she would not, but got further and further from me, and at last I could perceive her to take pins out of her pocket to prick me if I should touch her again; which seeing I did forbear ... So the sermon ended and the church broke up, and my amours ended also.' A year earlier the church had narrowly escaped destruction in the Great Fire, and to mark their gratitude the parishioniers commissioned a clock from Thomas Harris at a cost of £35. When this was set up over the street in 1671, it proved to be a sensation and people came from all over London to see it. Two giants, contained in a sort of Ionic temple supported by a black and gold bracket, strike the bells on the quarter hour, turning their heads in an action similar to the famous figures on the clock in St Mark's Square, Venice. Oliver Goldsmith alludes to the sight in *The Vicar of Wakefield* and Charles Dickens mentions it in *Barnaby Rudge*. The clock also features in William Cowper's descriptive lines taken from *Table Talk* (1782):

> *When Labour and when Dullness, club in hand*
> *Like the two figures of St Dunstan's stand*
> *Beating alternately in measured time*
> *The clockwork tintinnabulum of rhyme.*

In 1829, when the old church was finally demolished after a number of eighteenth century alterations and repairs, the clock was purchased by the Marquess of Hertford. However, in 1935 it was bought back by Lord Rothermere and reinstated outside the fine new Gothic Revival church which was built by John Shaw and completed by his son in 1833. It is constructed in brick with a handsome south tower of yellow Ketton stone. The upper part of the tower is octagonal with tall unglazed windows giving a 'lantern' effect, and topped by pinnacles. The statue in stone of Queen Elizabeth (c.1586) and the figures of King Lud and his sons,

all preserved from the old church, come from Ludgate.

Inside, the octagonal theme is repeated, with recesses on all eight sides, the altar and chancel being to the north. An early eighteenth century icon screen, placed here in 1966, separates the north-west chapel, which is used for Romanian Orthodox worship, from the rest of the church. The altar and reredos, intricately carved in oak, are early seventeenth-century and come from Antwerp. Many monuments from the old church remain, including one 'To the Memory of Hobson Judkin, Esq. ... The Honest Solicitor.'

St Dunstan's was damaged in 1944 when its lantern was set on fire, but was restored in 1950. It is now a Guild Church.

◆

ST ETHELBURGA-THE-VIRGIN WITHIN BISHOPSGATE Bishopsgate, EC2

This tenacious little building, which has survived the Great Fire and two World Wars, is probably the only Anglican church in the kingdom to bear this dedication. Opinions differ as to the saint's identity, but she was very likely the daughter of Offa, the eighth-century King of Mercia. The church was first mentioned in the thirteenth century. From 1366 until the Dissolution of the Monasteries it was in the patronage of the nearby convent of St Helen's by which it was rebuilt in the fifteenth century. After its annexation by the Crown, St Ethelburga's was allotted a parish of just three acres.

From the sixteenth century, to boost parish funds, St Ethelburga's was flanked on each side by shops which almost obscured its west front. When, in 1932, these were removed to widen the pavement, there was revealed a modest façade in ragstone, repaired at the top in brick, with a fourteenth-century doorway standing underneath a fifteenth-century window. Rising above it is an attractive eighteenth-century square bell-turret in two stages, crowned by a weathervane dating from 1671.

The modest interior consists of a nave and south aisle leading to the chancel and Chapel of St George. It is much enhanced by the modern rood

RIGHT St Dunstan's in the West

loft and delicately wrought chancel screen by Sir Ninian Comper, whose careful restoration in 1912–14 ameliorated some unharmonious Victorian innovations. A simple west gallery today replaces the former 1629 south gallery, installed, according to George Godwin (1839), 'only for the daughters and maidservants of the parish to sit in'. This was swept away in the nineteenth century. An interesting feature is the stained glass which includes four modern windows by Leonard Walker (1928–30), three of which depict episodes of Hudson's voyage to the East via the North Pole, and one in commemoration of W. F. Geikie Cobb, Rector from 1900 to 1941. An early incumbent was John Larke, friend of Sir Thomas More, who was hanged in 1544 for refusing to take the Oath of Supremacy.

There is great charm and pathos about this humble little church, wedged in between two huge, latterday office buildings, and it is accentuated by the small, secret garden, hidden away behind it. It became a Guild Church in 1954, and is the smallest church in the City, even smaller than the parish church of St Clement's, Eastcheap.

RIGHT St Ethelburga-the-Virgin

BELOW St Giles's Without Cripplegate

ST GILES'S WITHOUT CRIPPLEGATE
Barbican, London Wall, EC2 (1545-50)

The gate referred to in the dedication existed before the church. The name may have come from the Saxon word 'crepel', meaning covered way, or it may have alluded to the cripples who gathered here and of whom St Giles is patron saint. The first small place of worship on this site stood on swampy ground just outside the City Wall. It was built around 1090 by Alfune, associate of Rahere, who shortly afterwards founded the priory of St Bartholomew. It was enlarged and rebuilt no fewer than three times during the fourteenth century, and then again between 1545–50 after being nearly destroyed by fire. In 1665, the parish, which by now had become large and fashionable, was ravaged by the Plague. According to the records there were more victims here than in any other parish, possibly because, according to John Stow, the parish pump lay 'near unto the parsonage on the west side'. At least, however, in the following year St Giles's escaped the Great Fire and survived, albeit with numerous alterations and restorations, until the Second World War when it was reduced to a shell. It was restored by Godfrey Allen and reopened in 1960 as parish church to the Barbican development.

The exterior is mainly Victorian refacing and

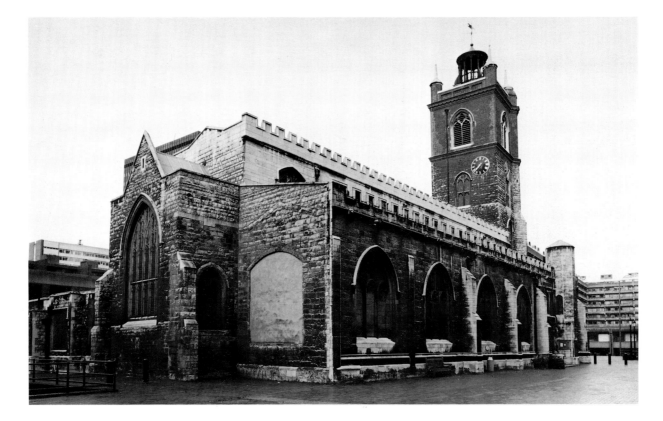

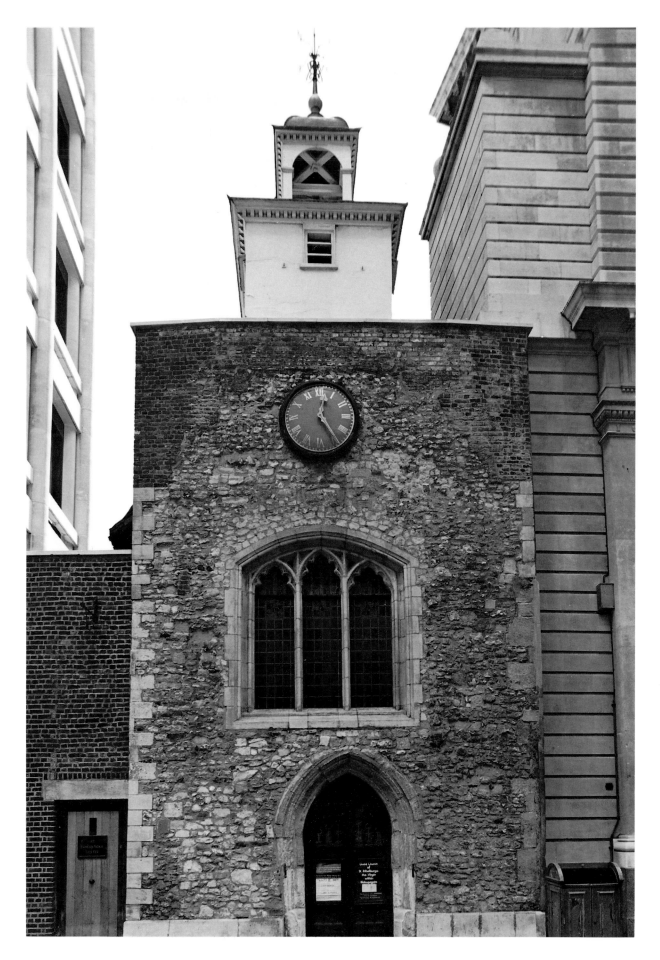

castellation, but the tower, constructed of earlier stone, retains its brick upper stage, built in 1682. It is topped by a little wooden cupola which replaced the former turret and pinnacles, The large interior is a rectangle with nave and aisles of seven bays reconstructed in the Perpendicular style. The furnishings are mostly modern, although the organ is eighteenth-century and, together with the font, came from St Luke's, Old Street, which was closed in 1959.

Numerous great names are encountered in the history of this church: John Foxe, author of *The Book of Martyrs*, was buried here in 1587, Sir Martin Frobisher, admiral and hero of the Spanish Armada, in 1594. A stone in the chancel floor marks the place where, in 1674, John Milton was interred. The story goes that his grave was opened in 1793, his hair and teeth offered for sale, and his remains exhibited for a few pence. He is also commemorated by a bronze statue in the south aisle. There is a memorial to John Speed, historian and cartographer, who died in 1629. It was in this church that Shakespeare attended his nephew's baptism in 1607, and here that Oliver Cromwell married Elizabeth Bourchier in 1620. The painter, Holman Hunt, was baptised here in 1827.

St Giles's stands in a conspicuous position surrounded by a paved churchyard forming a focal point in the Barbican complex. The parish also incorporates that of St Luke's, Old Street, outside the City.

◆

ST HELEN'S, BISHOPSGATE
Great St Helen's, off Bishopsgate, EC3

This fine, medieval church, which has survived intact from the early thirteenth century, owes its dedication to Helena, mother of Constantine the Great, the first Roman emperor to become a Christian. According to legend he founded it himself but the first mention of a place of worship on this site was in the second half of the twelfth century. At that time it belonged to the Dean and Chapter of St Paul's who, in about 1210, granted one William, the son of a goldsmith, permission to found a Benedictine nunnery in the grounds. The nuns' chapel was built abutting the little parochial church, which was at the same time extended. This produced a highly original, double nave, down the centre of which ran a screen to separate the nuns

from the parish congregation. It does not seem to have been very effective, since in 1385 the sisters received a stern rebuke for their frivolities, which included the kissing of secular persons, wearing ostentatious veils and the excessive number of little dogs kept by the Prioress. Fifty years later the nuns were again called to order and warned not to indulge in revelry and dancing except at Christmas, and then only among themselves.

As early as 1374, two chantry chapels – one dedicated to the Holy Ghost, the other to Our Lady – had been built to the east of the transept; and by the sixteenth century many other alterations and additions to the church had been made. At the Dissolution of the Monasteries the partition between the naves was removed, leaving only a fifteenth-century arcade of four bays as a reminder of where the nuns' choir had been. In the 1630s this arcade was repaired and beautified at the expense of various Livery Companies, and escaped unscathed in the Great Fire. Although it was added to and repaired several times during the eighteenth and nineteenth centuries, the essential fabric of the medieval church is unaltered. The thirteenth-century west front has great charm. It is formed of symmetrical halves, the north being the nuns' old nave, the south the former parish nave. The two are joined together beneath an embattled, undulating string course which, as Elizabeth and Wayland Young put it, 'provides a long eyebrow over the two west windows'. Above rises a small central bell-turret which was added in the seventeenth century.

The interior, while not very large, conveys an impression of space and opulence. There are splendid seventeenth-century carved door-cases to the south-west and west doors, and the many magnificent monuments testify to the wealth and patronage of past City merchants. In contrast, the south windows are plain and the roofs are of simple, low-pitch, tie-beam design.

In the north wall can be seen a night staircase for the nuns, an Easter Sepulchre and below it a squint. There is an outstanding seventeenth-century pulpit, richly decorated with a large canopy. The black and red marble font dates from 1632. In the chancel is a rare wooden sword-rest bearing the date 1665; also in the chancel are thirteen fifteenth-century choir-stalls originally in the nuns' choir. The monuments are so numerous

RIGHT St Helen's, Bishopsgate

ST JOHN IN THE WHITE TOWER
Tower of London, Tower Hill, EC3

The Chapel of St John is enclosed within the massive walls of the White Tower, that great Norman keep which, lying at the heart of the Tower of London, was built for William the Conquerer by Gundulph, Bishop of Rochester. Its seeming impregnability was called into question when, in 1381, Wat Tyler's rebels forced an entrance and abducted from the chapel Archbishop Sudbury with three others whom they found at prayer before the altar. Their victims were taken to Tower Hill where they were beheaded. Nearly 200 years later, in 1553, the chapel was used by the luckless Lady Jane Grey during her incarceration, both as queen and prisoner, in the Tower; and in the following year, her cousin, Mary Tudor, was married here by proxy to Philip II of Spain. During the reign of Charles II, St John's, for centuries the scene of royal devotions, was converted into a repository for state records, and continued thus until the nineteenth

ABOVE St Helen's, Bishopsgate

RIGHT St John in the White Tower

FAR RIGHT St Katharine Cree

as to have earned for St Helen's the title of the 'Westminster Abbey of the City'. Civic dignities from the past throng the church in marble effigy. Among them, an early fourteenth-century mayor, Adam Frances, is buried here. John Stow records of him that 'he procured an Act of Parliament that no known whore should wear any hood or attire on her head except red or striped cloth of divers colour'. A later Lord Mayor, Sir John Spencer, is commemorated with his wife by a spectacular monument north of the south entrance. He died in 1609, leaving nothing to charity nor dowering his daughter who, it is said, was abducted by the Marquess of Northampton in a bread basket. The parish includes that of St Martin Outwich.

century when it was restored for worship.

This small, bare chapel is one of the most impressive pieces of Norman architecture in England. It is of solid stone with a tunnel vault and groin-vaulted aisles. Heavy round piers with primitive decoration on the capitals carry the unmoulded arches which in turn support the gallery. Gallery and aisles, in a composition of touching simplicity, curve round the apse. From time to time there have been superficial renovations, but these have not affected the basic noble structure of the ancient stonework. Uniquely safeguarded from deterioration, St John's survives unspoiled and virtually unchanged after 900 years. Free Church services are held here on Sundays.

◆

ST KATHARINE CREE
Leadenhall Street, EC3 (1628–30)

'Cree' is a corruption of Christ. The first church here, known as 'St Katherine de Christ Church at Alegate', was built in about 1280 by the Augustinian Priory of the Holy Trinity within Aldgate on the edge of the Priory cemetery, in order that the canons 'be not disturbed by the presence of the laity at the services'. It did not last long and was rebuilt early in the fourteenth century; the present tower was built in 1504. St Katharine's was given full parish status in 1414. After the Dissolution of the Monasteries, the Priory church was offered to the parishioners in place of their own, which stood on a valuable site in Leadenhall Street, but they refused the offer, according to John Stow, 'having doubts in their heads about the afterclaps', and the monastic church was pulled down.

In 1628–30 St Katharine's was rebuilt, keeping the tower, and the new church was consecrated in 1631 by William Laud, then Bishop of London. The ritual he used at this ceremony was later decried as Popish and held against him at his trial in 1644. The new place of worship escaped the Great Fire and, as Pepys recorded, 'was resorted to by the Corporation' when the other churches were destroyed. It also escaped unscathed in the Second World War and its survival, more or less intact, provides an important example of a rare period of church building as, apart from the 1504 tower and its cupola added in 1776, the church is almost entirely Jacobean.

The windows are square-headed, the large west window being thinly pedimented. A sundial on the south wall, dating from 1706 is inscribed '*Non sine Lumine*'. The interior is light, of six bays resting on Corinthian pillars carrying rounded arches, unusual for the time. The clerestory with pilasters above follows the late Perpendicular style. There is no division between nave and chancel and the side aisles are now boxed in for offices. The plaster ceiling is very beautiful, groined and ornamented, and displaying seventeen coloured bosses bearing the arms of City Livery Companies. A square-framed wheel window at the east end symbolises the toothed wheel on which St Katherine was tortured. The octagonal marble font was donated by the Gayer family in 1646. Sir John Gayer, Lord Mayor in that year, also endowed the annual Lion Sermon in gratitude for his escape from a lion in Syria in 1643. When confronted by the beast, he had fallen to his knees in prayer and had been left unmolested. The organ, by Father Smith in 1686 and rebuilt by Father Willis in the nineteenth century, is in its finely carved original case, on fluted columns of oak.

Leading from the bapistry into the vestry is a

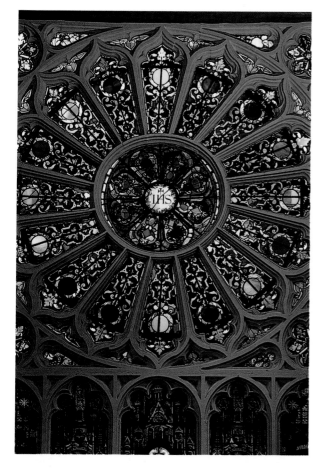

ABOVE AND LEFT St Katharine Cree, wheel window and ceiling detail

fine doorcase of 1693. The vestry opens into a charming and secluded garden which, in medieval times, used to be a setting for the enactment of miracle plays.

St Katharine Cree is the Guild Church for Finance, Commerce and Industry. Its former parish is included in that of St Andrew Undershaft.

◆

ST MARY WOOLNOTH
Lombard Street and King William Street, EC3 (Nicholas Hawksmoor, 1716-27)

There may been a pre-Norman church on this site, founded by one, Wulfnoth, to whom perhaps the dedication refers; or the name may have derived from the neighbouring wool market. Whatever its origins, a church here called St Mary Woolnoth was mentioned in 1273 and was rebuilt in about 1440.

The medieval building, although repaired by

Christopher Wren after the Great Fire, soon fell into decay; and by 1711 the parishioners were petitioning for a new church under the Fifty New Churches Act. Although the rebuilding of an existing church was not actually covered by the Act, their request was granted and Nicholas Hawksmoor was commissioned to design the new place of worship.

It was built between 1716–27 and Hawksmoor's inventive façade is so arresting that the awkward, wedge-shaped site on which the church stands is scarcely perceived. The west and principal front is on the corner of Lombard Street and King William Street. The massive lower story, containing an arched entrance beneath a semi-circular window, is heavily rusticated. Rising above it are Corinthian columns in the form of a square temple, and topping this highly original combination are two small square towers linked together by a short balustrade. The rustication continues round on the Lombard Street front which contains three Baroque arched niches. The side facing King

St Mary Woolnoth

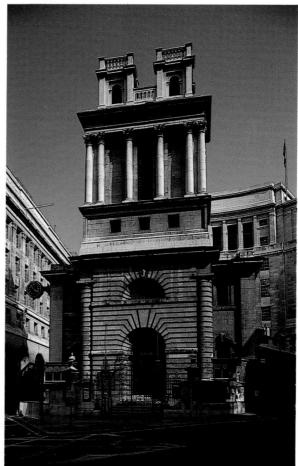

William Street is quite plain since it originally abutted onto another building.

The inside is a cube. One square is contained within a larger one, the central square being carried on four groups of three columns above the roof, forming a sort of clerestory lit by large semi-circular windows. The ceiling is blue, dotted with gilt stars. At the east end, in an arched recess, lies the altar, rather cramped under a black canopy, held up by twisted columns reminiscent of Bernini's *baldacchino* in St Peter's, Rome. Extensive alterations in 1875–6 by William Butterfield resulted in the removal of Hawskmoor's side galleries. But, as their richly carved fronts were considered too good to throw away, these were hung, in curious fashion, on the walls with their columns dangling beneath them. At the same time, Butterfield raised the floor of the chancel, covering it with polychrome tiles, took out the high pews and, most strangely of all, lowered the pulpit leaving the canopy on high. In addition to the small west organ attributed to Robert Dallam, there is now a large Victorian one occupying the north-east corner.

One of the former incumbents of St Mary's was John Newton whose sermons inspired William Wilberforce in his crusade against slavery. He also wrote the hymns *Amazing Grace, How Sweet the Name of Jesus Sounds* and *Glorious Things of Thee are Spoken*.

This is Hawksmoor's only City church. It has defied five attempts – including one by the City and South London Tube Railway – to demolish it, and continues to dominate the scene around it. It is now a Guild church. It is also the official City church for the Government of British Columbia.

◆

ST OLAVE'S, HART STREET
Hart Street, EC3

This is the only surviving church of five dedicated to St Olaf, the Norwegian king who supported Ethelred the Unready against the Danes in 1014. It was first mentioned in 1222 as 'St Olave towards the Tower'. Later in the same century the nave was lengthened to take in an ancient well, and this extension now forms the crypt of the present church. In the mid-fifteenth century, St Olave's was largely rebuilt with funds subscribed by Robert and Richard Cely, wealthy fellmongers

(skinners) of the parish. The plan was in the prevailing Perpendicular style with naves, aisles, clerestory and large east window. The low-pitched ceiling was rebuilt in 1632. In 1661 an outside staircase leading to reserved pews was erected on the south wall for the convenience of the Navy Office, then in Seething Lane, and this was often used by Samuel Pepys who regarded St Olave's as his own church. During the Plague in 1665, he recorded in his diary: 'July 26th: The Sickness is got into our parish this week; and is got endeed everywhere ... July 30th: It was a sad noise to hear our Bell to toll and ring so often today, either for deaths or burials; I think five or six times.' In the following year, anxious for the safety of the church during the Great Fire, he wrote: 'I durst not ask anybody how it was with us, till I came and saw it not burned. But going to the fire, I find, by the blowing up of houses and the great help given by the workmen of the King's yards, sent up by Sir W. Penn, there is a good stop given to it, as well at Marke-Lane end as ours.'

St Olave's survived the Great Fire only to be severely damaged during the Second World War. Its restoration, carried out by Ernest Glanfield,

ABOVE and LEFT St Olave's, Hart Street

in oak instead of pine. The church is beautifully cared for and very light. Among the furnishings is a splendidly carved pulpit from St Benet, Gracechurch and communion rails dating from the seventeenth century. The precise date of the sword stands is not known but their decorative ironwork is impressive. There are a number of interesting monuments, perhaps the most touching being the memorial with a bust to Pepys' wife, Elizabeth, who died in 1669. His own death in 1703 was not commemorated until the nineteenth century when a monument, designed by Sir Arthur Blomfield, was placed at the site of the old Navy pews in 1882. The bodies of husband and wife are buried beside the Communion table. To the left of the altar is a memorial to Peter Capponi, a Florentine gentleman who died of the plague; also to the left are two red-robed figures kneeling in prayer, 'Paule and Andrew Bayninge Esquire', dated 1610.

The arms of the Clothworkers' Company, whose annual service is held here, are displayed in a south aisle window. One of the very few medieval churches still remaining in the City, St Olave's is still a parish church. The parishes of All Hallows Staining and St Katherine Coleman were added to it in 1870 and 1921 respectively.

was completed in 1954, and a dedication stone, laid by King Haakon of Norway, links its past with its present. It remains unspoilt, a typical fifteenth-century church built in ragstone with a south-west tower. The bell-turret was enlarged after the war and a south porch added. The Navy pews were removed by the Victorians and an inscription marks the old entrance to them. A garden has now replaced the former churchyard which was described by Charles Dickens in *The Uncommercial Traveller* as 'one of my best beloved churchyards which I call the churchyard of Saint Ghastly Grim ... It is a small, small churchyard with a ferocious strong spiked iron gate like a jail. This gate is ornamented with skulls and crossbones larger than life, wrought in stone.' The gateway with its grisly adornments still forms the entrance to the garden and church.

Inside, the walls and most of the arcades are original; so, too, is the 1662 vestry with its delightful stuccoed ceiling. The 1632 roof was destroyed in the bombing and the present replica was rebuilt

ST PETER AD VINCULA
Tower of London, Tower Hill, EC3

A chapel to St Peter ad Vincula (in chains), standing at the north-west corner of the Tower's Inner Ward, is mentioned in 1210 when its use was intended mainly for the garrison and prisoners. In 1241, under Henry III, it was repaired and beautified as was its neighbour, St John in the White Tower, but unlike St John's it was rebuilt at the beginning of the fourteenth century by Edward I. A fire in 1512 resulted in another rebuilding, and the present chapel dates mainly from this time although there have been subsequent additions and restorations.

It is a long, low, flint building with a small brick tower at the west end topped by a charming, slender lantern; the windows are three-light below depressed arches. Nave and aisles are defined by slim columns and the roof is flat-pitched with original tie-beams. The organ, one of the oldest in the City of London, was made in 1679 for the Chapel Royal at Whitehall by Father Smith and transferred to St Peter's in 1890. Restored in 1853 and subsequently, it has still some original pipes in place. The Tudor font was broken in four pieces during the Commonwealth and concealed in the memorial to Sir Richard Cholmondley, Lieutenant of the Tower. It was rediscovered only in 1876, when it was restored to its rightful place. Other custodians of the Tower are commemorated here, and beneath the pavement lie a phalanx of Tudor and Stuart notables who, having incurred their Sovereigns' displeasure lost their lives: Archbishop Fisher and Sir Thomas More, 1535; Anne Boleyn, 1536; the Countess of Salisbury, 1541; Katherine Howard, 1542; Thomas, Lord Seymour, 1549; his brother, Edward, Lord Protector Somerset, 1552; the Duke of Northumberland, 1553; his son, Lord Guilford Dudley and daughter-in-law, Lady Jane Grey, 1554; the Earl of Essex, 1601; the Duke of Monmouth, 1685; and the Jacobite Lords of the 1745 uprising. Macaulay thought that 'in truth there is no sadder spot on earth' than St Peter's. Services are held here each Sunday for the residents of the Tower.

RIGHT Temple Church

BELOW St Peter ad Vincula

TEMPLE CHURCH
Inner Temple Lane, EC4

Temple Church takes its name from the Order of the Knights Templar, founded in Jerusalem in 1118 to protect Christian pilgrims in the Holy Land. The Order spread rapidly and in 1128 some of its members came to England where they established a church in Holborn. This was built with a rounded nave modelled on that of the Church of the Holy Sepulchre in Jerusalem or upon the Dome of the Rock. The Templars later moved to the present site where, in 1185, according to an inscription in the entrance, the round nave was consecrated by Heraclius, Patriarch of Jerusalem.

Throughout the next century the Order flourished, becoming so wealthy and powerful that at its dissolution in 1312 by Pope Clement V there were many eager contenders for its possessions. Eventually these were transferred to the Knights Hospitallers, a rival Order, amid such opposition in England that the Hospitallers did not assume ownership of the Temple until 1338. In the meantime it was administered by the Crown and leased to a series of tenants. At the Reformation, when it reverted to the Crown, two law societies, which had acquired the tenancy under the Knights Hospitallers, were allowed to remain and in 1608 were

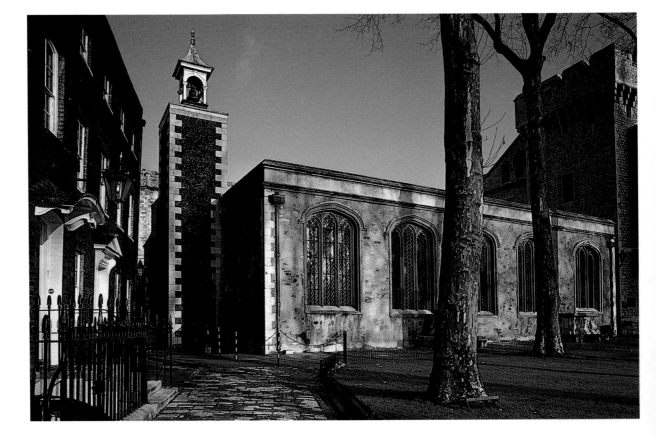

granted the freehold by James I. The lawyers' church, from which their own names derive (Inner and Middle Temples) is not subject to the jurisdiction of the Bishop of London but is under the direction of a Master appointed by the monarch. The Master from 1585 to 1591 was Richard Hooker, the famous divine, whose Calvinist reader, Walter Travers, drew crowds to hear his contentious afternoon sermons. According to Isaak Walton, 'The forenoon sermon spake Canterbury, and the afternoon Geneva.' The round nave, or the Round as it was called, seems to have been used as a waiting room for clients, and there were a number of shops against the south wall of the church. The Temple itself sometimes served as a committee room for the House of Commons.

Although the Temple Church was only slightly damaged in the Great Fire, Christopher Wren was consulted about repairs and recommended refurbishment with wainscotting, whitewash, box pews, pulpit and screen, and an organ. The choice of the organ in 1683–4 lay between instruments by Renatus Harris and Father Smith, the two law societies being divided in their preference. Purcell and John Blow played on Smith's organ and the Queen's organist on Harris's in a trial of excellence, but no conclusion was reached. The story goes that the choice was left to Lord Guilford, the Lord

Keeper of the Great Seal, but because he unfortunately died before declaring himself, his successor, Lord Chief Justice Jeffreys, decided in 1688 in favour of Father Smith. Renatus Harris was awarded £200 in compensation for his disappointment.

In a sweeping restoration of 1840–42 by Sydney Smirke and Decimus Burton the wainscotting and whitewash vanished and 'every ancient surface was repaired away or renewed', in the words of Walter Godfrey who, with his son, most beautifully restored the church after the Second World War.

The south side of the church, overlooking an open courtyard, is ashlar-faced and shows both the round of the nave to the left and the buttresses and triple lancet windows of the chancel to the right. Entrance from the west is through a richly decorated Norman doorway beneath a rib-vaulted Gothic porch. The circular nave at the centre of the church is defined by six grouped piers in Purbeck marble, supporting pointed arches rising to a triforium and above to a clerestory. The aisle windows are round-headed. The rectangular chancel is of a slightly later date, 1240, and is an exceptionally fine example of a Gothic hall-church with five bays and triple lancet windows. The vaulting throughout the church is original but the

Purbeck marble piers had all to be renewed after the War. In the south aisle there is an early double piscina, the use of which was prohibited in later times by Papal decree. A door in the north-west corner of the choir leads to the 'Penitential Cell' in which, it is said, Walter le Bachelor, Grand Preceptor of Ireland, starved to death. A twelfth-century undercroft discovered in 1950 is thought to have been a strong-room for the Knights Templar treasures; a grille on the stairway leading to it gives access to the remains of St Anne's Chapel where the rites of initiation into the Order probably took place. Effigies of knights lie around, mostly heavily restored, their inscriptions now illegible. A fully robed bishop, reposing in the south aisle with his feet upon a dragon, is one of the finest thirteenth-century monuments in the country. The deaths of Richard Hooker in 1600 and Oliver Goldsmith in 1774 are uncommemorated, their monuments having perished during the War, as did the contentious Father Smith organ which has been replaced by an instrument built for Lord Glentanar and presented by him to the Temple in 1953. A tradition of fine music here has been upheld in this century, and a recording of the choir in Mendelssohn's *Hear My Prayer* in which the young Ernest Lough sang 'Oh for the wings of a dove' became world-famous.

The Temple is one of the most important surviving churches of the Knights Templar, and is a remarkable instance of transition from pure Norman to pure Gothic. It retains its extra-parochial, and extra-diocesan status.

◆

CITY OF LONDON

THE CHURCHES OF
SIR CHRISTOPHER WREN

◆

ST ANDREW-BY-THE-WARDROBE
Queen Victoria Street, EC4
(Christopher Wren, 1685-93)

The early origins of this church are obscure, but its foundation may have been associated with the nearby Baynard's Castle which, demolished in 1884, was built soon after the Conquest. It is mentioned in a document of 1244, though the name Wardrobe was not attached to it until the second half of the fourteenth century when the royal stores, including ceremonial robes, were transferred from the Tower of London to a building adjacent to the church in Wardrobe Place. This building was destroyed in the Great Fire together with the medieval church, which was rebuilt by Christopher Wren in 1685–93.

St Andrew-by-the-Wardrobe was his last and cheapest church. Constructed of brick, originally 'finished or rendered over in imitation of stone',

but now of plain brick with stone dressings, it has a simple square tower of four stages with a straight top and parapet. The weather-vane came from St Michael, Bassishaw (demolished in 1900).

Inside, there are galleries on three sides carrying the decorated tunnel-vault over the nave, the west gallery having been added in 1774. Additions and alterations were made during the nineteenth century, many of them out of keeping with the simplicity of Wren's design. However, after severe bomb damage in the Second World War, the church was sympathetically restored by Marshall Sisson, who removed much of the Victorian work and renewed the church's original appearance. The former box pews have long since been replaced by benches and most of the furnishings have come from other churches. The organ was originally built in the eighteenth century, and was purchased for St Andrew's in 1961. The very fine pulpit, and the marble font and cover were originally at St

Matthew's, Friday Street, another Wren church which was demolished in 1883. There is some eighteenth-century stained glass at the west end; and the four modern windows on the south side are by Carl Edwards. The north aisle is partitioned off for offices, and the south aisle has been converted into a separate chapel.

The completion, in 1871, of Queen Victoria Street left the church in an elevated position. Its much reduced churchyard is now a landscaped garden, and the main approach is from the south through a pair of fine gates erected in 1902. St Andrew's serves an extended parish which includes six seventeenth-century parishes. It holds regular services and is, in addition, the headquarters of the Redundant Churches Fund and the Ancient Monuments Society.

◆

ST ANDREW'S, HOLBORN
Between Holborn and Holborn Viaduct, EC1
(Christopher Wren, 1684-90)

Founded in the thirteenth century on the site of two earlier places of worship, the medieval church of St Andrew, although surviving the Great Fire, had by then become dilapidated and was rebuilt by Christopher Wren in the 1680s. The parish was a big one and Wren designed the new church on a large scale, incorporating the west end of the original building with its Gothic arches and window, together with the lower part of the fifteenth-century tower. This he refaced in Portland stone in 1703, increasing its height with a heavy, ornate upper stage which contrasts oddly with the uncluttered appearance of the rest of the building.

The interior was altered in 1818, and again in 1871–2 by S. S. Teulon, who took, in his characteristic way, great liberties with the internal arrangements but whose dramatic effects with dark glass and polychrome decoration were completely destroyed in the bombing of 1941. Only his peculiar pulpit base survives. The tower and walls were left standing, however, and the building, thereafter sympathetically restored by Seely and Paget, was reopened in 1960. The interior is light and spacious with Corinthian columns rising from side galleries which are supported on wainscotted piers. The decoration is fresh and bright. There is a two-storeyed Venetian window at the east end with glass by Brian Thomas in eighteenth-

century style. The furnishings are all replacements of those destroyed in 1941, together with some from St Luke's, Old Street.

The organ case designed by Thomas Jacobsen, together with the white marble font and the pulpit, came from the Chapel of the Foundling Hospital (built 1742–52). So did the tomb to Captain Thomas Coram (died 1751), the Hospital's founder, which lies at the west end of the church. Opposite this is a memorial tablet to William Marsden who founded the Royal Free Hospital. The former large churchyard now consists of two small gardens to the north and west. The figures of two charity children executed in painted Coade stone can be seen from the west garden on the west front of the tower. These came from the parish school in Hatton Garden, built by Wren's master mason in 1696. In 1954 St Andrew's became a Guild church, its parish being divided between St Alban's, Holborn and St Bride's, Fleet Street.

LEFT St Andrew-by-the-Wardrobe

BELOW St Andrew's, Holborn

ST ANNE'S AND ST AGNES'S
Gresham Street, EC2
(Christopher Wren, 1677-80)

First mentioned in about 1467, the old church on this site was once called St Anne-in-the-Willows, although the sixteenth-century chronicler, John Stow, commented that there was 'no such void place for willows to grow more than the churchyard, where do grow some high ash trees'.

The small, red-brick church, built by Sir Christopher Wren between 1677–80 to replace the earlier building which had been almost completely destroyed in the Great Fire, retained what had survived of the fourteenth-century west tower. This is now capped with a bell-turret surmounted by a gilded weather-vane. A cement rendering applied to the walls in 1820–21 was removed when, after a period of neglect following the bombing of 1940, the church was restored to its original appearance by Braddock and Martin Smith between 1963 and 1966.

The interior design, used by Wren here and in two other City churches (St Mary-at-Hill and St Martin-within-Ludgate), derives from an Early Christian plan consisting of a central square containing a Greek cross. The ceilings are adorned with elegant plaster decorations and the groined vault is blue. The small interior, without stained glass or galleries, gives an effect of light and space, enhanced by the plain, part-panelled walls.

Among the furnishings, mostly acquired from other churches, the Royal Arms of Charles II came from St Mary's, Whitechapel. The black stained reredos contains paintings of Moses and Aaron which were originally in St Michael's, Wood Street. The post-war font is a copy of the former acquisition from St Mildred's, Bread Street but retains its original cover.

The gardens which have replaced the former churchyard provide a charming setting for this delightful little church which, since 1966, has served the Lutheran community. Special arrangements have to be made to see inside, although midday concerts are frequently held here. Services are held in Estonian and Latvian as well as in English.

RIGHT St Benet's, Paul's Wharf

BELOW St Anne's and St Agnes's

ST BENET'S, PAUL'S WHARF
St Benet's Hill, Upper Thames Street, EC4
(Christopher Wren, 1677-83)

St Benet is the abbreviated form of St Benedict, and the first mention, in 1111, of a church on this site refers to 'Sancti Benedicti super Tamisiam'. St Benet's has belonged to the Welsh people, almost without interruption, since 1320 when they were introduced into the neighbourhood by Edward II, although it was not until 1879 – after the church had been threatened with demolition – that, united with the parish of St Nicholas Cole Abbey, it was officially confirmed as the Welsh Episcopalian church in London, which it still remains. Since 1555 it has also been, by Royal Charter, the Chapel of the Royal College of Arms which stands across the road from it.

The early building was destroyed in the Great Fire, and the present delightful little church was built by Christopher Wren between 1677–83. It escaped damaged during the Second World War and has survived almost entirely unaltered despite restoration in 1836 and a serious fire in 1971 which

damaged part of the interior. Very small and almost square, St Benet's is most appealing to look at from the outside. It is built in dark red and blue brick reminiscent of the Dutch architecture of the period, and is embellished with plain stone quoins and ornamental swags over the rounded windows. The same design of brick and stone is repeated in the very pretty north-west tower, which is topped by a lead-covered cupola and short lead spire. The interior is equally captivating, with north and west galleries resting on Corinthian pillars, panelled walls and a flat ceiling. The original stone floor is inset with many slate monuments, and the church is very light and cheerful with heraldic banners hung all round. The altar was a gift from Charles II, whose carved and painted Royal Arms above the doorcase to the tower lobby are particularly fine. The altar table is an outstanding feature with an inlaid wooden top adorned by cherubs' heads and supported at the corners by angels instead of legs. The Communion rails, with scrolled twisted balusters, are perhaps by Jean Tijou, as is the sword-rest in the nave. Among the many monuments to heralds from the nearby Royal College of Arms is one to John Charles Brook, who was crushed to death by the collapse of a ceiling in the Haymarket Theatre on a royal occasion in 1797. There is also a small tablet which was put up on the east wall in 1878 to Inigo Jones, who was buried with his parents beneath the chancel of the former church and whose tomb was left undisturbed by Christopher Wren. The original memorial to him perished in the Great Fire.

Shakespeare referred to St Benet's in *Twelfth Night* when Feste utters these words: 'The Bells of St Bennet, sir, may put you in mind.' The novelist, playwright and magistrate, Henry Fielding, married his second wife here in 1747.

St Benet's is closed except for services.

◆

ST BRIDE'S, FLEET STREET
Bride Lane, Fleet Street, EC4
(Christopher Wren, 1671-8)

Until the beginning of the nineteenth century this church was dedicated to St Bridget, the sixth-century Irish saint who was believed to have been able to change well water into beer. It was no doubt in the hope she might do so again that the

St Bride's, Fleet Street

little place of worship, built by a well near the River Fleet, was dedicated to her. There had been at least one previous building on the site, indicated by the twentieth-century discovery of Roman remains, and several more churches followed the Saxon one.

In the fifteenth century a new building in the Perpendicular style was constructed by William Vyner, Warden of the Fleet Prison, to replace the former Norman church. This, dating from the late twelfth century, had played a secular as well as a religious role: from its tower had rung out one of London's four curfew bells. At about the same time Wynkyn de Worde, apprentice of William Caxton, brought his printing press to Fleet Street and set it up close to Vyner's new church, and in its wake there thronged to the neighbourhood many writers and poets. Among these were Dryden, Milton, Izaak Walton, Richard Lovelace and John Evelyn, all of whom were parishioners. Samuel Pepys, who, together with his eight brothers and sisters, was christened in the church,

has left an account of the difficulties concerning his brother Thomas's funeral here in 1664: 'And to the church and with the grave-maker chose a place for my brother to lie in ... But to see how a man's tombes are at the mercy of such a fellow, that for 6d. he would (as his own words were) "I will justle them together but I will make room for him" – speaking of the fulness of the middle Isle where he was to lie.'

Two years later St Bride's was completely destroyed in the Great Fire, and in 1670–75 another church by Christopher Wren was built upon the ashes. The celebrated steeple, also by Wren, was added in 1701–3. The shape of this, with its intricate octagonal stages, diminishing in size and topped by an obelisk, was so suggestive to a nearby pastry-maker, Mr Rich, that he became famous for his wedding cakes modelled upon it. Struck by lightning in 1764, the spire lost eight of its 234 feet, causing grave concern to George III who consulted – among others – the American, Benjamin Franklin, about a suitable lightning conductor. The King was advised to use a form with pointed ends, and his insistence upon blunt ends provoked such comments as 'good, blunt, honest King George'.

Throughout the centuries St Bride's continued to be associated with men of letters. The Society of St Cecilia held its annual music festival here and Dryden composed the ode 'Alexander's Feast' for its members. Samuel Johnson, James Boswell, David Garrick, Oliver Goldsmith, Joseph Addison, Alexander Pope and William Hogarth all lived within one hundred yards of the church, and the links with printers and journalists were legion.

Although gutted in the Second World War, the church retained its outer walls and was afterwards restored by Godfrey Allen with careful regard to Wren's designs. The interior has five bays with a slightly projecting chancel and a tunnel vault. This rises on arches carried by tall Tuscan double columns and is decorated with gilded rosettes. To the west can be seen the old minstrels' gallery. The floor is of black and white marble. Unfortunately the original seventeenth-century furnishings have been lost; but the new fittings are in the style of Wren and include a very fine oak reredos. The crypts house a fascinating exhibition of Roman and other relics illustrating the church's history, together with a wealth of detail concerning the vital and enduring contact that has been maintained between St Bride's and Fleet Street.

ST CLEMENT'S, EASTCHEAP, EC4
(Christopher Wren, 1683-7)

St Clement's is dedicated to the supposed third successor of St Peter as Bishop of Rome, the patron saint of sailors, who suffered martyrdom by drowning with an anchor round his neck.

The tiny church which stood here in medieval times was referred to in the thirteenth century as St Clement Candlewickstrate. It was completely destroyed in the Great Fire and was not replaced until the 1680s when it was rebuilt by Christopher Wren. In token of their gratitude the parishioners gave him a third of a hogshead of wine.

Like its predecessor, Wren's church is also very small although lofty in proportion. The walls follow the irregular site, giving a nearly triangular south aisle which is separated from the body of the church by two columns. The unassuming exterior is stuccoed except for the south-west tower, the upper part of which is in brick. Inside the church is equally plain except for the flat ceiling which is ornamented with gilded plaster. In 1872 William Butterfield carried out some drastic alterations, removing the south gallery, re-siting

St Clement's, Eastcheap

the organ and dividing the reredos into three. These changes were modified in 1933 by Sir Ninian Comper who reassembled and coloured the reredos. The fine 1695 Renatus Harris organ, enlarged but with its front casing intact, has been returned to its original position over the west door. Henry Purcell was organist here for a time.

In striking contrast to the modest appearance of the church, the pulpit is magnificent. Very large, with a big canopy, it is carved in oak adorned with cherubs and swags. The octagonal marble font dates from the seventeenth century.

This, the smallest parish church in the City, has an equally tiny garden with a single tree and a few rose bushes, a quiet little oasis surrounded by office buildings.

◆

ST EDMUND THE KING
Lombard Street, EC3
(Christopher Wren?, 1670-79)

Little is known of the origins of this church, the only one in the City which is dedicated to the martyred King of East Anglia. It is referred to in

the twelfth century as St Edmund Grasschurch, in allusion to the hay and vegetable market in which the church stood. The medieval building was completely destroyed in the Great Fire, and the church that replaced it in 1670–9 is ascribed to Christopher Wren but may have been designed by his assistant, Robert Hooke. Unusually, it faces north. The spire was added in 1706.

The narrow stone façade has three bays with arched windows and quoins. The south tower, which rises from the pedimented central bay, has a decorated cornice carrying an octagonal lead lantern. An attractive feature is the way in which the outer bays are linked with the steeple by concave pieces, a theme which is repeated in the concave spire above the lantern.

The interior is a plain rectangle with aisles having a flat ceiling with a semi-dome over the altar. It was rearranged in 1864 by William Butterfield, who, by judicious re-use of the original carved woodwork and other ornaments, succeeded in preserving the character of the old church. In particular, the pulpit is very fine, and the seventeenth-century font standing in the north-west corner is enclosed by a richly carved semi-circular balustrade. The impressive reredos includes in its six decorated panels the figures of Aaron and Moses painted by William Etty in 1833. In the

First World War, St Edmund's was damaged by a German bomb, fragments of which have been preserved.

It was in this church that Joseph Addison married the Dowager Countess of Warwick, his next-door neighbour, in 1716.

◆

ST JAMES'S, GARLICKHITHE
Garlick Hill by Upper Thames Street, EC4
(Christopher Wren, 1676-83)

There was mention of a place of worship on this site in 1170, when, according to John Stow, the dedication referred to the sale of garlic nearby. The church was rebuilt in 1320, and at that time the parish was evidently an important one since no fewer than six medieval Lord Mayors were buried there.

Destroyed in the Great Fire, it was rebuilt by Christopher Wren between 1676–83, the spire being added in 1714–7. During the nineteenth century there were a number of restorations, not all in accord with its Wren character. However, a further restoration by Lockhart Smith and Alex-

elegant carved pulpit with its balustred staircase, and the doorcases cut down to form the screen backs of the stalls. The church is also fortunate in its possession of a rare Bernard Smith organ of 1697 with its original front pipes, although there are some additions at the top of the casing. The beautiful chandelier made by Arnold Montrose in 1967 is based on an eighteenth-century model in the Wren chapel at Emmanuel College, Cambridge.

The parish of St James's now includes those of St Michael Paternoster Royal, St Michael's, Queenhithe, All Hallows the Great and Holy Trinity the Less. Seven Livery Companies hold their annual services here.

ABOVE Bernard Smith organ, St James's, Garlickhithe

LEFT St Edmund the King

RIGHT St James's, Garlickhithe

ander Gale after the Second World War – when the tower was refaced and the roof repaired from the ravages of death-watch beetle – removed the Victorian stained glass and returned the church to its former appearance.

The exterior is dominated by the plain square tower, above which rises a graceful steeple in three stages, very pretty and complex with columns and vases, the two upper stages being very small and topped by a weathervane. Inside it is lofty. The nave is of five bays formed by tall Ionic columns, and the deeply coved ceiling is furnished with clerestory windows which light the gilded plasterwork. The narrow aisles are lower than the nave and contain so many arched windows that at one time St James's was known as 'Wren's Lantern'. The east window has been replaced by a painting of The Ascension by Andrew Geddes, donated in 1815, which hangs over the altar. The ironwork is exceptionally fine; so too is the woodwork, much of which came from St Michael's, Queenhithe, demolished in 1875. Particularly notable are the

ST LAWRENCE JEWRY
Gresham Street by the Guildhall, EC2
(Christopher Wren, 1671-7)

This church is named after the saint who suffered martyrdom on a gridiron in the third century; the other part of the dedication refers to the colonization of this area by the Jews until they were expelled by Edward I in 1290.

The first mention of a place of worship here was in 1136 when it belonged to a French convent. From 1294 it was attached to Balliol College, Oxford in whose patronage it remained until 1957 when it became the Guild Church of the Corporation of London.

The medieval church appears to have been of handsome appearance, well endowed with stained glass. It was consumed in the Great Fire and its replacement, built by Christopher Wren between 1671–7, was also richly ornamented. Its interior was totally destroyed in the Second World War but, after careful restoration by Cecil Brown, it was reopened in 1957.

St Lawrence is in the form of a rectangle, cunningly adjusted to fit its irregular site. The stone-faced exterior is plain except for the east side which faces the approach to the Guildhall. This displays a fitting grandeur with Corinthian columns, large pediment, festoons and swags. The square tower, with obelisks at each corner, supports a tall steeple of fibreglass.

Inside the church is spacious, with one aisle divided by columns and with dark panelling round the walls. The ornamented ceiling is a replica of the original. A distinguishing feature of the former sumptuous interior was the magnificent woodwork which was all destroyed, as was Wren's irreplaceable little vestry, enchantingly decorated and containing paintings by Sir James Thornhill. However, the (mostly) modern fittings are handsome and in accord with civic dignity. A fine Noel Mander organ of 1956 has a case copied from that by Renatus Harris with late additions; there are eight beautiful chandeliers by Cecil Brown, and the modern stained glass by Christopher Webb, while not in the strict Wren tradition, adds colour and harmony. A carved oak screen separates the Commonwealth Chapel from the nave.

Among the notable visitors of the past were Sir Thomas More, who delivered a discourse here in 1501, and Samuel Pepys who attended divine service in 1664. He was impressed by the church but not by the preacher, There are many associations with City Companies. The Loriners and the Haberdashers hold annual services here, as do the Girdlers' Company with whom the tradition has lasted since 1180. It is also the church of the New Zealand Society who, each year, commemorate their National Day here.

Today, in addition to providing spiritual comfort to the Corporation, St Lawrence is used for talks and music recitals.

◆

ST MAGNUS THE MARTYR
Lower Thames Street, EC3
(Christopher Wren, 1671-76)

It is generally assumed that the martyr referred to was the Norwegian Earl of the Orkneys, who was canonized in 1135 and of whom there is a painted wooden statue on the south wall. However, in 1067 a stone church, standing on this site and bearing the name 'St Magnus', was bestowed upon Westminster Abbey by William the Conqueror, so the dedication may be to an earlier saint.

Little is known of the church in medieval times, although it is recorded that the parish received an annual levy from a chapel standing on the adjac-

LEFT St Lawrence Jewry

RIGHT Swordrest, St Mary at Hill

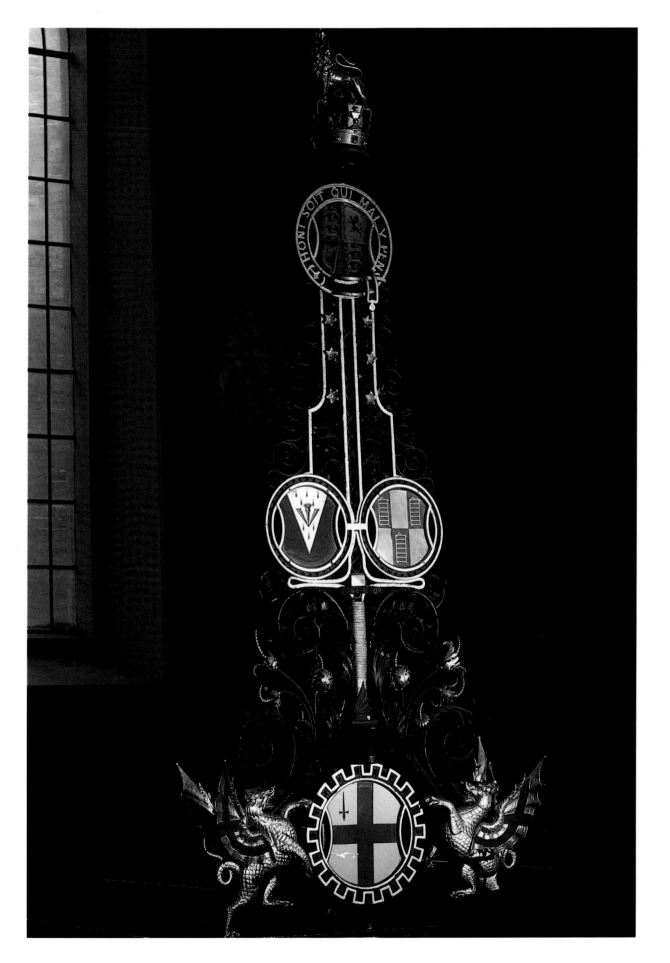

its tall steeple is still a prominent feature. Constructed in Portland stone, the square tower supports a large octagonal lantern and lead-covered dome, crowned by an obelisk spire.

Inside, a restoration in the 1920s by Martin Travers and later work by Laurence King has imparted an Anglo-Catholic flavour to the spacious Wren interior with the addition of a Lady Chapel. The striking white and gold decoration is enhanced by the many fine fittings, notable among which is the splendid reredos. The diagonally placed side altars, one made from a door-case, were assembled in 1924 by Martin Travers. There is a particularly impressive seventeenth-century pulpit with tester, and the organ has a case of 1712 by Abraham Jordan adorned with carvings of musical instruments. A splendid sword rest dated 1708 bears the Royal Arms of Queen Anne. Miles Coverdale, translator of the Bible into English and Rector here from 1564 to 1566, was buried in the southeast corner of the church. He was originally buried in St Bartholomew-by-the-Exchange, but his remains were brought to St Magnus's in 1841, together with the 1837 tablet on the east wall. The present windows in the south aisle are by Lawrence Lee. St Magnus's is still a parish church. The Coopers', Plumbers' and Fishmongers' Companies all hold their annual services here.

ABOVE St Magnus the Martyr

RIGHT St Margaret's, Lothbury

ent London Bridge to compensate it for loss of alms; and the master mason, Henry Yevele, who was responsible for Westminster Hall, founded a chantry in the church where he was buried in 1400. In the late fifteenth century 'priestis and clarkes in tyme of dyuyne service' were called to order for dallying in taverns and fishing in the Thames instead of attending to their duties. A victim of the Great Fire, the church was rebuilt by Christopher Wren in 1671–6, and in 1762 the aisles at the west end were cut back to allow for a footpath, which, running under the tower, provided access to the recently widened London Bridge. Further alterations to the north wall ensued to redress the balance of symmetry, and in 1782 the partial infilling of the north windows to make them circular completed the work. St Magnus's lost its pre-eminent position facing the bridge when the new London Bridge was built, further west in 1832. And it is now almost hidden from view by its huge neighbour, Adelaide House of 1924–5. However,

ST MARGARET'S, LOTHBURY
Lothbury, EC2
(Christopher Wren, 1686-90)

It is recorded that a certain Reginald was priest here in 1181, but little else is known about the early history of this church. According to John Stow, it was rebuilt in about 1440, but was devastated in the Great Fire. Some time after, between 1686–90, it was reconstructed by Christopher Wren, the tower and spire being added in 1698–1700. St Margaret's survived unscathed in the Second World War. It is constructed in Portland stone. When building it Wren followed the medieval plan and, as a result, the church is of an irregular, oblong shape with one aisle and the tower in the south-west corner. The walls are very plain. So also is the square tower, but the lead spire crowning it – an obelisk on a domed base – is very pretty.

The inside is dominated by a spectacular display of seventeenth-century furnishings, many acquired in the nineteenth century from those demolished churches whose parishes were added to that of St Margaret's. Taking pride of place is the Wren chancel screen which stretches from wall to wall. It consists of a central entrance capped by an open segmental pediment below which hangs a great carved eagle with spread wings. On each side are four open divisions, separated by delicate two-strand wooden spirals, looking just like fragile sticks of barley-sugar, which support subsidiary pediments. The effect is so compelling that it almost diverts attention from the huge canopy overhanging the pulpit. This is a marvellous composition of cherubs, birds, fruit and flowers, which also comes from All Hallows, although the pulpit itself is indigenous. The reredos in the chancel is yet another sumptuous piece, flanked on each side by paintings of Moses and Aaron which date from 1700 and were acquired from St Christopher-le-Stocks. The communion rail from St Olave Jewry echoes the barley-sugar theme with its fine twisted balusters. There are two superb sword-rests at the ends of the south and north pews.

The south aisle has been screened off to form a small chapel which is also replete with treasures. The charming little stone font, often attributed to Grinling Gibbons, has an attractive wooden cover, another gem from St Olave Jewry, as is the simple reredos. On the south side of the door leading to the chapel is a fine bust by Joseph Nollekens dating from 1795. The Scientific Instrument Makers' Company – whose arms are displayed in a stained glass window in the chapel – hold their services here, and the church is also used for recitals of music. Now incorporating seven parishes, its full designation is now St Margaret Lothbury and St Stephen's, Coleman Street with St Christopher-le-Stocks, St Bartholomew-by-the-Exchange, St Olave Jewry, St Martin Pomeroy, St Mildred Poultry and St Mary Colechurch.

◆

ST MARGARET PATTENS
Rood Lane, Eastcheap, EC3
(Christopher Wren, 1684-7)

The dedication may indicate a benefactor, or it may refer to the high wooden soles or pattens commonly worn in the Middle Ages to protect the

ABOVE St Margaret Pattens

LEFT St Martin-within-Ludgate

feet from mud. There is a notice in the vestibule requesting women to remove their pattens before entering the church.

Although there is mention of a wooden chapel here in 1067 and a reference to 'St Margaret de Patins' in 1275, nothing is known of the medieval church or the reason for its demise in 1530. Shortly after this date however, a rood, or cross, was erected in the churchyard for the collection of offerings to build a new church which was completed in 1538. The new building did not survive the Great Fire and was rebuilt by Christopher Wren between 1684–7, the tower being added a few years later.

The outside is quite plain. The square tower at the north-west is finished with a balustrade and four needle-shaped pinnacles, one at each corner, a motif which is repeated in the lead-covered spire which is capped with a ball and vane. The interior, also plain, has a flat ceiling, round clerestory windows and galleries to the north and west, the northern one having been made into offices since the Second World War. There are, however, some exceptionally fine furnishings which include two canopied pews of great rarity, one of which has the initials 'CW' with the date 1686 inlaid in its roof. It may have stood for Christopher Wren who attended this church, but equally may have meant 'Churchwarden'. There is also a beadle's pew to the north of the altar, at present (1987) obscured by posters. The excellent reredos contains a seventeenth-century painting of The Agony in the Garden by Carlo Maratta. The seventeenth-century octagonal font is decorated with four cherubs' heads and has an eighteenth-century cover. Another outstanding piece is the Stuart Royal Arms, one of two in the church, the only example in the City to date from the reign of James II. Over the altar in the chapel in the north aisle is a Della Robbia plaque; also in this chapel is a line of wooden pegs attached to the panelling at the west end. Among the monuments is one to Sir Peter Delme, Lord Mayor and Governor of the Bank of England, sculpted by Michael Rysbrack; another is to Charles I with a wooden plaque inscribed 'Touch not mine anointed'. It was erected here by James Fish, Rector from 1866–1907, who instituted an annual service to the memory of the King on the anniversary of his execution. An earlier Rector, Thomas Wagstaffe, was deprived of his living for refusing to swear allegiance to William III.

The Pattenmakers' Company and the Basket-makers' Company hold their annual services here. Baskets used to be made in Rood Lane by Flemish immigrants. St Margaret's is now a Guild Church serving as a Christian Study Centre.

◆

ST MARTIN-WITHIN-LUDGATE
Ludgate Hill, EC4
(Christopher Wren, 1677-84)

Lud Gate, traditionally said to have been built by King Lud in 66 BC, was one of six great gates leading into medieval London. Together with the other gates, it was demolished in 1760. The first authentic mention of the church was in 1174. It is known to have been rebuilt in 1437, but was destroyed in the Great Fire. The new church was built by Christopher Wren between 1677–84, a few feet further to the north, thus incorporating part of the City Wall in its west end. The site is an awkward one on sloping ground, wider from north to south than from east to west, with the south side aligned to the street. Wren's solution was to construct a vestibule within the south entrance, separated by coffered arches and screens from the main body of the church which thus became square-shaped.

The south façade is extremely attractive. It is of three bays in Portland stone, the central bay consisting of the slightly projecting tower. This is linked to the other two by large angled scrolls which emphasize the three segment-headed windows below, while at the same time leading the eye upwards to the beautiful slender spire which, with its octagon, ogee dome, lantern and lead-sheathed obelisk, provides a satisfying contrast to the great dome of St Paul's in the background.

Inside it is rather dark. The square interior holds a smaller central square carried by four tall Corinthian columns raised on high plinths. The design is similar to that of St Anne and St Agnes and St Mary at Hill. The small west gallery, the only one now remaining, is reached by stairs with twisted balusters. It contains a little organ of 1845 by Theodore Bates of Ludgate Hill. A rare furnishing is the double chair for churchwardens; it has a cane seat and back and dates from 1690. On the south side there are three truly magnificent doorcases giving access to the vestry and vestibule. One of these (possibly by Grinling Gibbons) is particularly richly carved with cherubs' heads, garlands and Corinthian pilasters. In the vestry a brass monument of 1586 from St Mary Magdalene, Old Fish Street, perpetuates the memory of Thomas Berry, fishmonger, who left '12 penie loves to 12 poor foulkes every Sabathe day for aye'.

St Martin's is now a Guild Church. It is also the Regimental Chapel of the Middlesex Yeomanry and the Chapel of the Honourable Society of the Knights of the Round Table. The parish is attached to the Church of the Holy Sepulchre, Holborn.

◆

RIGHT St Martin-within-Ludgate

ST MARY ABCHURCH
Abchurch Lane, EC4
(Christopher Wren, 1681-6)

The place of worship which stood on this site in the twelfth century was referred to as St Mary Abchurch, possibly meaning 'Up Church', since it stood on slightly rising ground. It belonged, at that time, to the Priory of St Mary Overie, now Southwark Cathedral. In the fifteenth century, however, the patronage was transferred to Corpus Christi College, Cambridge, with which it still remains. The early church, complete with bell-tower and murals, was destroyed in the Great Fire and rebuilt by Christopher Wren between 1681–6. Since then this, one of the prettiest of Wren's churches, fortunate in having been spared serious damage in the Second World War, has been singularly little altered.

It stands in a quiet position flanked by a cobbled courtyard. Its demure red brick (formerly stuccoed) exterior with hipped roof, stone quoins and delightful little steeple on an ogee-domed base, is reminiscent of St Benet's, Paul's Wharf. Inside, the similarity ends. Light floods in from an enormous window on the south side of the church revealing a square interior covered by a huge, shallow dome (over 40 feet across) which, without aid of buttresses, rests on arches springing from the white walls and on one pillar. The fine painted ceiling was executed around 1708 by William Snow, who lived in the parish and may have been a friend of Wren. Below is some of the most beautiful woodwork in the City. The great altarpiece with its profusion of trailing fruit and flowers was designed by Grinling Gibbons, and much of it carved by him. There is, for once, a signed receipt of 1686 to authenticate it as Gibbons's own work. The original pulpit steps still mount to William Gray's fine canopied pulpit, and the marble font was made in 1686 by another craftsman, William Kempster, brother of Christopher Kempster, master mason of the building. The cover for it is by William Emmett who also carved the doorcases and the Royal Arms of James II. The richly carved pews are all original, although those on the south side have been dispossessed of the dog kennels which used to lie under them. The organ is by Noel Mander, but the carved oak front dates from 1717 and came originally from All Hallows, Bread Street. Two Lord Mayors have donated sword-rests to commemorate their mayoralty and a third, Sir Patience Ward, who held office in 1680, is

ABOVE St Mary Abchurch; RIGHT St Mary Aldermary

remembered in a fine memorial erected at his death in 1696. St Mary Abchurch is now a Guild Church with close associations with the Fruiterers' Company whose arms are displayed in the great south window.

◆

ST MARY ALDERMARY
Queen Victoria Street, EC4
(Christopher Wren, 1681-1704)

There is mention of a church on this site in about 1080. The name 'Aldermary' may mean 'Elder-mary' indicating that it is older than the nearby Norman foundation of St Mary-le-Bow, but it may derive from 'altera' (the other) Mary.

The early church was rebuilt in about 1510 by the then Lord Mayor, Sir Henry Keeble, who died before it was finished in 1518. Work started again in 1530 on the tower, but the project was only finally completed after further benefactions in 1629. Although damaged in the Great Fire, most of the new tower survived the flames which destroyed the rest of the building and was incorporated into the new church built, rather belatedly, by Christopher Wren in 1681–1704. Perhaps he had not welcomed the commission which, apparently, had carried the stipulation that St Mary's should be reconstructed in its former image to comply with the terms of a £5,000 legacy. Although there is no documentary evidence of this condition, it seems that Wren abided by it and the church was rebuilt in Gothic style, but with some interesting innovations.

The outside is faced in stone, and the tower, which was renewed about twenty years later, follows the original ladder-pattern. It culminates in four pinnacles, formerly in stone, but since 1962 reconstituted in fibreglass. At first sight the interior seems unequivocally Perpendicular with pointed arches and shafted piers. But a glance

upwards corrects the impression, as the beautiful plaster fan vaulting in the nave and aisles is unprecedented in a parish church of this period. In addition, the large rosettes sunk in shallow saucers are another untraditional feature, as is the plaster decoration in the spandrels of the arcade.

In the nineteenth century the church suffered a punitive restoration in which the interior was stripped of most of its beautiful seventeenth-century woodwork. All that remains today of the original furnishings is the marble font donated in 1627 and enclosed with twisted baluster rails, a fine late seventeenth-century pulpit decorated with garlands and cherubs' heads but minus its tester, an impressive wooden sword-rest fixed to the south-west pillar of the nave which dates from 1682, and a splendid doorcase at the west end which came from St Antholin's, Budge Row after its demolition in 1875–6. Among the monuments is one, by the younger John Bacon, adorned by urn and swag, to Margaret Bearsley (d. 1802).

St Mary Aldermary is now a Guild Church and its parish has been added to that of St Mary-le-Bow. The Skinners' Company holds its annual service here.

◆

ST MARY AT HILL
Lovat Lane, EC3
(Christopher Wren, 1670-76)

A record of 1177 concerning a place of worship adjacent to the town house of the Abbots of Waltham Abbey refers to 'Sanctee Mariae Hupenhulle', an illusion to the rising ground on which it stood. The building was substantially enlarged towards the end of the fifteenth century, but was badly damaged in the Great Fire. It was not completely burned down, however, and the tower, together with what remained of the north and south walls, was incorporated into the new church built by Christopher Wren between 1670 and 1676. The spire was added in 1695. Almost a hundred years later, in the 1780s, the tower with its battlements was rebuilt not in stone, as specified by the surveyor, James Gwilt, but in red brick, while, at the same time, the west wall was renewed in yellow brick. The Gothic windows which had survived from the fifteenth-century church were finally jettisoned in the 1820s when the north and south walls were rebuilt by James Savage. Under his

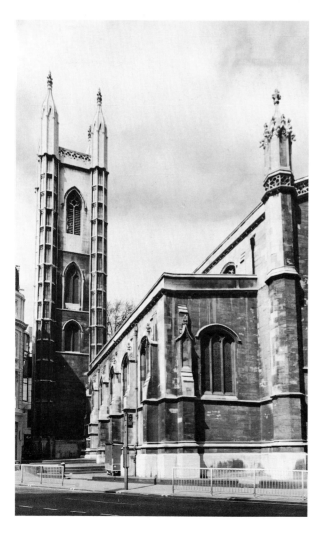

a white background, reminiscent in its delicacy of the work of Robert Adam. The furnishings are quite remarkable, the mid-nineteenth-century carving by William Gibbs Rogers harmonizing so closely with the original woodwork that it is hard to distinguish between them. However, the canopied pulpit, complete with a long and elaborate staircase, the reading-desk and rector's pew all bear the date 1849, and the lion and unicorn guarding the way to the altar are inscribed VR. The richly carved organ-case is also possibly by Rogers, the lectern and the chancel stalls are certainly so. Of the original woodwork, the Wren altar piece is particularly fine, and there is a complete set of box pews, unique in the City. Of the six superb sword-rests (see picture on page 59), two commemorate William Beckford, twice Lord Mayor and father of the writer and collector who built Fonthill Abbey.

A past incumbent from 1892–1926 was Prebendary Wilson Carlile, who founded the Church Army and whose trombone, which accompanied so many services in the church, is preserved in the vestibule.

LEFT St Mary at Hill

RIGHT St Mary-le-Bow

ST MARY-LE-BOW
Cheapside, EC2
(Christopher Wren, 1679-80)

The first known place of worship here was called St Mary Newchurch, perhaps to distinguish it from St Mary Aldermary nearby. The later name of le-Bow is thought to derive from the round arches in the Norman crypt.

Its early history was eventful. In 1091 the roof was blown off in a great gale and several people were killed. In 1196 William Fitz-Osbert, a seditious tailor, took refuge in the tower and had to be smoked out. In the next century, in a drama of 1284, a goldsmith, one Laurence Ducket, was murdered in the church where he had sought sanctuary, and St Mary's was closed for a time while the sacrilege was purged. There was another fiasco in 1331 when a wooden framework beside the church, used for viewing purposes, collapsed during a tournament attended by Queen Philippa, wife of Edward III. Fifty years earlier the tower had subsided into the market place, killing several

direction there was further work in 1848–9 when the decoration was altered and some new furnishings added. Most of the Victorian stained glass introduced at this time was removed in the 1960s during renovations by Seely and Paget who replaced it with translucent glass. Threatened with demolition by a projected railway extension in 1879, St Mary's was reprieved, and later the church survived the Second World War without damage.

The unassuming, plain brick outside conceals a splendid interior lit by a variety of windows high and low. The Greek cross design, similar to that employed by Wren in St Anne and St Agnes, has been incorporated here into an irregular rectangle. Four fluted columns carry vaulting which supports a shallow-domed central square. The four corners between the arms of the cross have low flat ceilings. Across the west arm is a fine gallery resting on carved pillars. The Victorian plasterwork of the dome and ceilings is coloured in blue and gold on bystanders, and not until 1512 was it completely rebuilt. The whole building was demolished, however, in the next century after damage in the Great Fire to be replaced by the present church, designed by Christopher Wren and completed in 1680, the most expensive of his City churches.

The magnificent steeple juts proudly upward, separated from the modest red brick church behind it by a vestibule. Although St Mary's was badly damaged in 1941, its external appearance today is much the same as when it was first built, the steeple having been taken down, strengthened and replaced stone by stone in an admirable post-war restoration by Laurence King. The large square tower gives way to a square bell-tower, complete with balustrade and pinnacles, above which a circle of free-standing columns support a top stage of twelve colonnettes, the whole edifice being surmounted by an obelisk from which flies the weathervane – an enormous copper dragon

made by R. Bird in 1679. On the second storey of the north face is a small balcony commemorating the medieval balcony which was built to replace the wooden structure, formerly used by royalty as a grandstand. On the north and west fronts of the tower are two elaborate doorways with cherubs and putti carved above the keystone, each framed by a rusticated arch, giving access through a vestibule to the interior of the church. Here, a wide nave with very narrow aisles leads without division into the chancel. The altar is free-standing, the seating versatile and the modern furnishings uncluttered. The attractive stained glass was made by John Hayward in the 1960s. The famous Bow Bells, commemorated in legend and nursery rhyme, which in the Middle Ages rang out the curfew, were recast in 1954 and now sound their peal a semitone lower.

St Mary-le-Bow is flanked to the west by a large paved courtyard in place of its former churchyard and embraces nine parishes in addition to its own.

◆

ST MICHAEL'S, CORNHILL
St Michael's Alley and Cornhill, EC3
(Christopher Wren, 1670-72;
Tower, Nicholas Hawksmoor, 1715-22)

The name Cornhill probably derives from the corn market held there, according to John Stow, since 'time out of mind'. A Saxon church stood on the site, and an early record refers to the living being given to the Abbot of Evesham in 1055. In 1503 this passed to the Drapers' Company by whom it is still held. Stow, whose forebears were buried here, was fond of St Michael's about which he wrote: 'This has been a fair and beautiful church, but of late years ... greatly blemished by the building of low tenements on the north side thereof.' He added that it had 'on the south side thereof, a proper cloister, and a fair churchyard'. In this churchyard a tent was erected in 1657 for the sale of coffee, a coffee house – the first of its kind in London – having recently opened in St Michael's Alley. The present little churchyard stands on the site of the cloister and now, as then, St Michael's is cluttered by surrounding buildings.

From early times there was a tower from which, in the fifteenth and sixteenth centuries, the curfew used to sound. The tower survived the Great Fire and was included in the new church built by Christopher Wren between 1670–2. Shortly afterwards, however, it was deemed unsafe, and in 1715 work was begun on a new tower probably also to designs by Wren. Held up for lack of funds, the project was not completed until 1722, and the finished work is generally ascribed to Nicholas Hawksmoor. It rises 130 feet high and is constructed on Gothic lines topped by four pinnacles. The addition of a porch, intended to introduce a more accurate Gothic character, was part of an 1859 restoration by Sir George Gilbert Scott. He gave the church a Gothic Revival face-lift from which it has never really recovered, although the effect was modified when, in 1952, gold and white paintwork replaced the Victorian polychrome on the walls. At the same time, Scott banished almost all the original furnishings and commissioned William Gibbs Rogers to carve the replacements. The windows in the aisle contain Italian tracery which he thought appropriate, and the pink marble reredos with which he replaced the one by Wren still presides over the altar. Black and white tiles cover the floor of the chancel and the ceilings throughout are vivid blue. The only seventeenth-century furnishings left are the altar table and the

font. The beautifully carved pew ends, pulpit and lectern are all by William Gibbs Rogers. One remarkable adornment, not cast out in 1859, is the gilded wooden Pelican in Piety dating from 1775. This stands on a pedestal at the west end of the church.

St Michael's has suffered considerably from its Victorian treatment. It is still a parish church. The Drapers, the Merchant Taylors, the Master Mariners and the Guild of Air Pilots and Air Navigators all hold their annual election-day services here. The parish of St Benet Fink, which was demolished in 1845–6 to make way for the new Royal Exchange, was incorporated into that of St Michael in 1906, together with the parish of St Peter Le Poer.

◆

ST MICHAEL PATERNOSTER ROYAL
College Hill, EC4
(Christopher Wren, 1686-94)

Rosaries with beads indicating that paternoster, the Lord's Prayer, was to be said were once sold near here in Paternoster Row. The 'Royal' in the name derives from La Reole near Bordeaux which used to supply the City merchants with wine.

There was a reference to 'St Michael of Paternosterchierch' in 1219. In about 1409 the church was rebuilt by Sir Richard Whittington, four times Lord Mayor of London, who lived next to St Michael's and was buried there in 1423. He also founded a College of Priests (from which College Hill takes its name) to pray for him and his family. This was dissolved in 1540. When the church succumbed to the Great Fire, the monument to Sir Richard burned with it. The whereabouts of his body is now a mystery, the last search for it, in 1949, having revealed only a dead cat.

St Michael's was rebuilt by Christopher Wren between 1686 and 1694, the steeple being added later. William Butterfield carried out a restoration in 1866 but left the fine woodwork undisturbed. A further restoration, by Elidir L. W. Davies, designer of the Mermaid Theatre, took place after bomb damage in 1944; and the church was reconsecrated in 1968. The newly formed Whittington Garden lies to the south of it.

LEFT and RIGHT St Michael's, Cornhill

St Michael's is a modest little stone church with round-headed windows the keystones of which are in the form of cherubs' heads. A south-west corner tower rises squarely to an extremely pretty small turret. This, with its eight circling columns supporting a small octagon with a domed top and weathervane, provides a delightful contrast to the otherwise plain exterior.

The simple rectangular interior still contains some of the original furnishings including the altar-piece, canopied pulpit, doorcases and lectern. The lectern, together with a very fine brass chandelier dated 1644, came from All Hallows the Great. The legend of Dick Whittington and his cat is commemorated in stained glass in one of the south windows, although the cat was never associated with Whittington until the legends accumulated round his name almost two hundred years after his death in 1423. There is also some fine modern stained glass by John Hayward in the east windows.

St Michael's is now a Guild Church. Its parish has been transferred to St James's Garlickhythe, and the tower and west end are used as the headquarters of the Missions to Seamen.

ST NICHOLAS COLE ABBEY
Queen Victoria Street (between Friday Street and Distaff Street), EC4
(Christopher Wren, 1671-7)

St Nicholas, familiar to generations of children as Santa Claus, is also the patron saint of travellers and seamen. The meaning of Cole Abbey is obscure, but it is thought to be a corruption of Cold Harbour, the medieval word for shelter or lodging-house. The first mention of St Nicholas's was in a letter of Pope Lucius II dated 1144. Later, in a charter of 1272, it is referred to as '*Sci Nichi retro fihstrate*' or 'St Nick's behind Fish Street'. During the reign of Elizabeth I, according to John Stow, a wealthy fishmonger subscribed £900 for a tank, fed with water piped from the Thames, to be set up against the north wall 'for the care and commodity of the Fishmongers in and about Old Fish Street'. During the seventeenth century the patronage was held for a time by Colonel Hacker

RIGHT St Nicholas Cole Abbey

BELOW St Michael Paternoster Royal

who signed the order for Charles I's execution and was later beheaded as a regicide.

The medieval church which was destroyed in the Great Fire was one of the first to be rebuilt by Christopher Wren. It cost £5,042. 6s. 11d., and among the accounts submitted was one for 'Half a pint of canary for Dr Wren's coachmen, 6d.' Some 200 years later, during the laying of the London underground, the foundations were disturbed. A subsequent vent gave rise to smoke and fumes which blackened the church and earned for it the nickname 'St Nicholas Cole Hole Abbey'. It was burned out in 1941 and the restoration by Arthur Bailey was completed in 1962.

It is a simple rectangular church with a balustrade around the top. The windows are round-headed under straight hoods, and the low northwest tower supports a quaint little steeple, its concave form, adorned by round and oval lunettes, rising to a small balcony above which flies a weathervane in the form of a ship from St Michael's, Queenhythe (demolished 1876). Inside it is perfectly plain, without divisions, below a flat ceiling. A carved screen at the west end separates the rest of the church from the organ gallery, vestry and

tower. The east end is adorned by some impressive plasterwork garlands over the altar. Some of the original furnishings, rescued during the war, include a very beautiful font cover (the font is a copy), fine pulpit and communion rails and the Royal Arms of Charles II, all dating from the seventeenth century, and a magnificent eighteenth-century brass chandelier. The stained glass in the three east windows is by Keith New and dates from 1962.

An amusing early episode in the church's history concerns the vicar, Thomas Sowdley, who under Edward VI took a wife, the first incumbent of St Nicholas's to do so. So great an embarrassment was she to him during the subsequent reign of Mary Tudor, that he is said to have sold her to a butcher.

St Nicholas's has long links with the Bowyers' Company who hold their biannual commemorative service here. It is now leased to the Free Church of Scotland.

ST PETER UPON CORNHILL
Cornhill (between St Peter's Alley and Gracechurch Street), EC3
(Christopher Wren, 1677-81)

Like its neighbour, St Michael's, this church is built upon one of the two hills (the other is Ludgate) on which Roman London was established. An ancient tablet in the vestry affirms that St Peter's was founded by King Lucius in 179 AD, and that it was the 'chief church of this kingdom' for 400 years before St Augustine transferred it to Canterbury. This is highly doubtful, but it is true that St Peter's is of great antiquity and was highly esteemed in the Middle Ages. Indeed, its Rector had precedence over all others in the annual Whit Monday procession to St Paul's Cathedral. The first mention of the church was made in the eleventh century, and early records refer to many chantries and altars. Late in the fourteenth century, a Brotherhood and Guild of St Peter's, associated with the Fishmongers' Company, was founded here for religious observances, and early in the next century one of the four City grammar schools was established here. This was refounded

in 1447 by Henry VI and continued into the eighteenth century. In addition, an ancient library was attached to St Peter's, but this was dispersed in the early sixteenth century. Even as late as Victorian times, the mystique surrounding St Peter's preserved it from either demolition or amalgamation under the 1860 Union of Churches Benefices Act.

The old place of worship was all but completely destroyed in the Great Fire. However, the brick base of the tower survived and formed part of a new church, built by Christopher Wren between 1677 and 1681. In spite of some Victorian restoration, St Peter's has not been much tampered with. The outside walls are stuccoed and the principal façade to the east is impressive. It is of two storeys, the lower one containing five arched windows separated by pilasters, the upper having one arched, and two circular windows, the whole being crowned by a pediment. The storeys are linked, Italian fashion, by curved pieces. The simple south wall overlooks the small churchyard, while to the west rises the red brick tower, topped by a small dome, lantern and obelisk. These are sheathed in green copper which blends harmoniously with the yellow stucco of the walls and the red brick of the tower.

The interior is of five bays with a tunnel-vaulted nave. The pillars which divide the bays are skilfully distorted to conceal the irregular shape of the site. It is enhanced by the excellent furnishings of which the most striking is the Wren chancelscreen, twin to that in St Margaret's, Lothbury, but unique in its original setting. It is beautifully executed with slender shafts dividing the sections and a centrepiece curving up, flanked by wide, fluted pilasters. In front are the Royal Arms of Charles II. The canopied pulpit of the same period is very fine, but was lowered in the nineteenth century. The octagonal font is of 1681; so, too, is the gallery and case housing the organ, although the instrument itself was rebuilt by William Hill in 1840. The original keyboard by Father Smith is now in the vestry. In 1840 it was played by Mendelssohn who declared it to be the 'finest in London' and bestowed on it his autograph.

George Borrow, author of *Lavengro*, was married here in 1840. Charles Dickens, in *Our Mutual Friend*, has left the following account of the churchyard:

ABOVE St Peter upon Cornhill

RIGHT St Stephen's, Walbrook

They emerged upon the Leadenhall region, and Charlie directed them to a large paved court by the church, and quiet too. It had a raised bank of earth about breast high in the middle enclosed by iron rails. Here, conveniently elevated above the level of the living, were the dead and the tombstones, some of the latter droopingly inclined from the perpendicular, as if ashamed of the lies they told.

All that remains today is a small paved courtyard with two large plane trees and a few benches. St Peter's is still a parish church. It has associations with the British Sailors Society, and the Poulters' Company hold their annual service here.

◆

ST STEPHEN'S, WALBROOK
Walbrook (between Bond Court and St Stephen's Row), EC4
(Christopher Wren, 1672-9)

First mentioned in about 1096, St Stephen's takes its name from the stream which used to flow through the City into the Thames. The early church stood on its west bank and was succeeded, early in the fifteenth century, by a second church, built on the east side of Walbrook, which was later destroyed in the Great Fire. The present church, also on the east side, was constructed by Christopher Wren between 1672–9, the spire being added considerably later, in 1717. St Stephen's was badly damaged during the Second World War, restored afterwards by Godfrey Allen and reopened in 1954.

The exterior of Wren's church is plain except for the steeple which has been described by Nikolaus Pevsner as 'amongst Wren's most playful spires'. Set well back from its surrounding balustrade, the tower, in square form with three columns at each corner, rises to a second stage which is crowned by a little lantern surmounted by a weathervane.

St Stephen's is entered from a doorway to the south of the tower. Steep steps lead up through a lobby into one of Wren's most celebrated interiors. In a simple rectangle, sixteen Corinthian columns are disposed, both longitudinally – emphasizing the passage of the nave and aisles – and in a circle around the central open space. This space, which

forms the heart of a Greek cross within a square, is overhung by a great cream-coloured dome supported on eight arches carried on as many columns. A marvellous effect of spatial harmony is created by the intricate crosses, squares and arches all leading up to the dome, the whole being lit by the lantern above and by windows throughout the church. The mosaic floor was removed in 1986–7. Most of the furnishings, saved from destruction during the war, are original. These include the woodwork of the west lobby with a magnificent organ gallery above, the reredos and the pulpit, complete with decorated canopy and staircase with twisted balusters. The font is of stone with a beautiful octagonal cover. Henry Pendleton, incumbent in the sixteenth century, was the famous 'Vicar of Bray'.

The *Critical Review of Publick Buildings in London* of 1734 affirmed that St Stephen's was 'famous all over Europe, and justly reputed the masterpiece of the celebrated Sir Christopher Wren'. When it was first built, the churchwardens voted that 'twenty guineas in a silk purse' should be presented to Dr Wren or his lady, in gratitude for 'his great care and extraordinary pains in contriving the design of the Church'. St Stephen's has recently been restored by Robert Potter at a cost of well over £1 million. In February 1987 the ten-ton marble altar by Henry Moore was deemed a suitable ornament for the church by the Court of Ecclesiastical Causes Reserved which overturned a previous decision by the London Diocesan Consistory Court.

◆

ST VEDAST ALIAS FOSTER
Foster Lane, EC2
(Christopher Wren, 1670-73)

Little is known about the early history of this church or how it came by its curious name. St Vedast was the sixth-century Bishop of Arras who baptised Clovis, Emperor of the Franks, in the Christian faith. It seems likely that his name, in the popular Flemish equivalent Vaast, developed into Fauster – thence Foster. Certainly, John Stow, writing in 1598, referred to 'St Fauster's, a fair church lately newly built'. After the Great Fire, St Vedast's was left with its walls still standing, and these were incorporated into Christopher Wren's new church, built between 1670 and 1673,

ABOVE St Vedast alias Foster

LEFT St Stephen's, Walbrook

the steeple being added later. St Vedast's was a victim of the bombing during the Second World War, but the tower and steeple survived. Subsequently restored by Stephen Dykes Bower, the church was reopened in 1962.

The east wall displays a transition from rubble masonry to brick and is probably medieval; the east and west windows, both mullioned with transoms, seem also to belong to an earlier period. About the steeple, however, there can be no doubt: this is a fine Baroque spire, slim, beautiful and austere, set in wonderful contrast against the great rounded shape of nearby St Paul's. It is one of Wren's few stone spires and is unusually integral with its tower from which it rises, white and square, the first stage concave, the second convex, both with clusters of projecting pilasters at the angles, to a grooved obelisk embellished with a weathervane. Inside, a simple rectangle with arcades of Tuscan pillars and arches has a flat ceiling, adorned with gold and silver paintwork. The pews have given way to college-type seating and the single south aisle has been screened off from the rest of the church to form the separate Chapel of St Mary and St Dunstan. It is adorned with a collection of furnishings from other churches. The organ, by John Harris (1731), was restored by Noel Mander in 1960–1. The eighteenth-century casing came from St Bartholomew-by-the-Exchange and the octagonal pulpit from Wren's All Hallows, Bread Street, demolished in 1878. The carved font and cover once belonged to St Anne and St Agnes. The altar-piece, originally at St Christopher-le-Stocks, came here by way of Great Burstead Church in Essex. It was here that Robert Herrick, the finest of the seventeenth-century English lyric poets, was baptised in 1591.

St Vedast's is the only surviving parish church in an area which once contained twelve. Its churchyard has been replaced by a small garden known as Fountain Court. In it, on the south wall, a tablet inscribed to Major Vladimir Vassilievitch Petropavlovsky (1888–1971) 'Soldier of the Tsar, of France, of England' bears the words: 'This was a man'.

◆

In addition to these surviving churches, four of Wren's towers still exist in the City. These are Christ Church, Newgate Street, EC1 (completed 1704); St Mary Somerset, Upper Thames Street, EC4 (1686–94); St Augustine-with-Faith, Watling Street, EC4 (1680–7); St Dunstan-in-the-East, Idol Lane off Great Tower Street and St Dunstan's Hill, EC3 (1697). Wren's tower of All Hallows, Lombard Street (1686–94) has been recreated at All Hallows, North Twickenham (see p. 168).

◆

CITY OF
WESTMINSTER

◆

AGHIA SOPHIA, GREEK ORTHODOX CATHEDRAL
Moscow Road, W2 (1877-9)

Aghia Sophia, the Holy Wisdom, was built in 1877–9 for the Greek community whose numbers had swelled since the early nineteenth-century war of independence. The design by Sir George Gilbert Scott's second son, John Oldrid Scott, is in the Byzantine style, much praised by Ruskin and just then coming into vogue. The plan is orthodox with a Greek cross below a large central dome.

The interior is spacious and very richly furnished and decorated with marble inlay and coloured woods. The screen which shuts off the sanctuary is particularly elaborate with icon paintings by Professor Ludwig Thiersch of Munich who had spent several years teaching in Athens. The vaults and dome are covered with mosaics which were so much admired in 1893 by the critic of the *Builder* that he declared them to constitute 'one of the most important pieces of church decoration in London'.

ALL SAINTS, ENNISMORE GARDENS SW7
(Lewis Vulliamy, 1846-9)

All Saints, designed by Lewis Vulliamy, was built between 1846–9, and now belongs to the Russian Orthodox Church. The Italianate west front, complete with campanile, was added in 1892 by C. Harrison Townsend (who designed the Horniman Museum in Forest Hill). The interior, formed like a basilica, is galleried on three sides with tall iron Corinthian columns and has a small clerestory. The decoration is by Heywood Sumners, one of the leading exponents of the Arts and Crafts movement.

ABOVE All Saints, Ennismore Gardens

Aghia Sophia

RIGHT Aghia Sophia

ALL SAINTS, MARGARET STREET
Margaret Street, W1
(William Butterfield, 1849-59)

All Saints stands on the site of the former Margaret Chapel which was built in about 1760 and was used for a time for sectarian worship before it eventually became a centre for the Oxford Movement in 1839 under Frederick Oakey. Oakey's successor, Upton Richards, set up plans to replace the Chapel with a model new church which would provide for the needs of High Church ritual. His scheme was sponsored by the Ecclesiological Society, whose representative, A. J. Beresford Hope, expressed a desire for something more than an ordinary parish church. His wish was gratified by William Butterfield, then aged thirty, who produced one of the first great examples of High Gothic Revivalism, passionately conceived, properly planned and solidly constructed.

All Saints was built between 1849 and 1859 with a clergy house and choir school attached. These stand with the church, all massed together on a small awkward site, dominated by an enormously

All Saints, Margaret Street

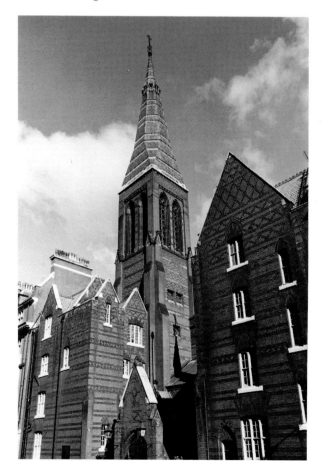

tall steeple, clad at the top in slate. The theme of the dark slate is repeated in the black brick adornments which are in dramatic contrast to the dusky red brick walls of the church and ancillary buildings.

The church is entered through two doorways, set very close together, both rich in ornament. Inside, a three-bayed nave, 70 feet high, leads through a wide arch into the chancel. Marble, granite and alabaster combine with the powerful Perpendicular structure in obedience to Ruskin's maxim, 'beauty and effect of colour shall arise from construction and not from super addition'. But there is a great deal of colour: in tiles above the arcades, on the floor of the chancel and on the wall of the north aisle, where the tale of the Nativity is depicted in brilliant shades of green and maroon. The entire east wall forms a backdrop for the altar which, conforming to Tractarian practice, is raised on high. The reredos is composed of tiers of red and blue saints under gilded canopies, and the frescoes above, originally painted by William Dyce (1854–9), were replaced with a set of paintings by Sir Ninian Comper in 1909. There is an abundance of rich stained glass.

As an architectural exposition of a creed, All Saints is one of the most important churches of its time. According to G. E. Street, 'this church is not only the most beautiful, but the most vigorous, thoughtful and original among them all.' It remains Butterfield's masterpiece.

◆

ALL SOULS, LANGHAM PLACE
Langham Place, Regent Street, W1
(John Nash, 1822-4)

All Souls, one of the two churches in London designed by John Nash, was built between 1822–4 as part of his masterly scheme of town planning for the West End. It was constructed on the bend of Langham Place which forms a hiatus between Regent Street and Portland Place. And, so that the church should be visible to each, Nash placed it diagonally to the bend, fronting it with a circular portico which takes up the view in both directions. Ingenious as this was, his architectural mix of Classical balustraded colonnade, carrying a smaller colonnade mounted by a sharp spire, was thought outrageous, and Nash was publicly

ABOVE All Souls, Langham Place

RIGHT Chapel Royal

CHAPEL ROYAL
St James's Palace, SW1 (1530s)

The Chapel was part of the Palace of St James's, built by Henry VIII on the site of a former hospital for maiden lepers dedicated to St James the Less. The outside is obscured by the surrounding Palace buildings. The interior is T-shaped with five box galleries inserted in the walls, the south one being the Royal Closet and another containing the organ. Most of the decoration is nineteenth-century, but the ceiling is original, in blue, pan-elled with octagons and crosses. There is a splendid display of gold and silver plate, mainly of the seventeenth century.

The Chapel is renowned for its tradition of music. Among the early organists were Thomas Tallis, William Byrd and Henry Purcell. Naturally, it has been the scene of innumerable royal occasions. It was here that Charles I received Communion on 30 January 1649 before going to his execution; here that countless Stuart and Han-overian royal babies have been baptised; and it was in this Chapel that George IV was unwillingly married to Princess Caroline of Brunswick in 1795;

lampooned. A cartoon of the time by Cruikshank shows the architect impaled on the metal spike atop his steeple; Nash's riposte was that criticism had exalted him.

There have been a number of repairs and alter-ations to the church since it was built, the most recent in the 1970s when the foundations were excavated and the floor raised to provide a hall beneath for social activities. The space revealed displays the inverted brick arches which were exposed during the reconstruction.

The church is entered by a round vestibule into a galleried hall, with an opening at the east end for the sanctuary. The altarpiece, a painting by Richard Westall, was a gift from Nash's patron, George IV, and provides a significant focal point in the otherwise open space. The coved ceiling, carried on marble Corinthian pillars, is flat with gilt panels, and the decoration is in gold and grey. The furnishings are modern and include a metal altar, pulpit and lectern. The 1913 organ, rebuilt by Willis in 1951, was further rebuilt in 1978 by Harrison & Harrison of Durham, using the mahogany casing designed by Nash.

ABOVE Chapel Royal; RIGHT French Protestant Church

LEFT All Saints, Margaret Street

that Queen Victoria was married to Prince Albert in 1840, and their grandson George V (then Duke of York) married Princess May of Teck in 1893.

◆

FRENCH PROTESTANT CHURCH
Soho Square, W1 (Sir Aston Webb, 1893)

Sir Aston Webb maintained that this church was the favourite of his buildings. It was commissioned in 1881 by descendants of those Protestant refugees who had found asylum in England during the sixteenth century. Permission to buy the site had to be obtained from the Attorney-General which caused some delays in building; and the church was not completed until 1893. The façade, in black brick and black and brown terracotta, has four storeys with a gable and lantern. The interior consists of nave, aisles and an apse. The aisle

vaults are unusually designed with a series of saucer domes, ribs, bosses and a central glass eye. The clerestory has three part openings and a surrounding balcony projects above the arcade.

◆

GROSVENOR CHAPEL
South Audley Street, W1 (1730)

The Grosvenor Chapel, probably designed by Benjamin Timbrell or possibly by Francis Price, was completed in about 1730 as an estate chapel for the new Grosvenor Square development. In the words of Sir John Summerson, 'it resembles more than any other surviving London church the kind of thing which emigrant builders were putting up across the sea in New England'. The exterior is modest in yellow brick with round-headed windows. At the front, a central bell-turret, surmounted by a bluish spire, rises above a four-column Tuscan porch. Inside there are three galleries supported on square pillars with Ionic columns above. The original simplicity of design has been enriched by Sir Ninian Comper who,

shown pilasters on the lower stage of the tower, but the parishioners, thinking this niggardly on the part of the Commissioners, subscribed the extra cost of the present columns and urns. The handsome stone façade has a shallow Ionic portico below a balustrade. The columned tower rises in two stages, one square, one circular capped by a cupola. The round apse was added in 1878 by Somers Clarke, and the external pulpit is part of a memorial to Canon William Cadman, the rector from 1859–91, whose preaching drew large crowds.

Among the distinguished parishioners of the nineteenth century were the Duke of Wellington, J. M. W. Turner and William Gladstone; Florence Nightingale and Lord Roberts of Kandahar were both regular members of the congregation.

In the First World War Holy Trinity was used as an air raid shelter, and later, while the church was still in regular use, part of the crypt was rented by Allen Lane to store early editions of Penguin Books. In the 1950s, the parish was reunited with St Marylebone's, and Holy Trinity became the Headquarters of the Society for Promoting Christian Knowledge. There is now a bookshop in the nave, but there is still an altar, and services are occasionally held in the chancel.

early in this century, installed an open screen of tall columns at the end of the nave, creating a Lady Chapel out of the former chancel. The pulpit and communion rails are contemporary with the chapel.

The chapel, which became a chapel of ease to St George's, Hanover Square in 1831, also forms the headquarters of the inter-denominational Association for Promoting Retreats, with offices in Liddon House next door. Buried here are the parents of the Duke of Wellington, Lady Mary Wortley Montagu and John Wilkes.

◆

HOLY TRINITY, MARYLEBONE
Marylebone Road (north side by Albany Street), NW1 (Sir John Soane, 1824-8)

Holy Trinity, standing fairly close to, but on the opposite side of the road from St Marylebone Parish Church, was built between 1824–8 to help serve the expanding population in the area. It was designed by Sir John Soane as one of the 'Waterloo' churches. In his original plan he had

CHURCH OF THE IMMACULATE CONCEPTION Farm Street, W1
(J. J. Scoles, 1844-9)

Familiarly referred to as 'Farm Street', the Church of the Immaculate Conception is the English headquarters of the Society of Jesus. In 1844 the Jesuits, enabled by the 1829 Act. of Catholic Emancipation to build their own place of worship, commissioned J.J. Scoles to design for them a church which was to stand on a site that had once been part of Hay Hill Farm. The church was completed in 1849 in a flamboyantly Decorated-Gothic style, the *pièce de résistance* being the high altar and reredos by Augustus Welby Pugin. This stands beneath a nine-light window (inspired by one similar in Carlisle Cathedral) which is answered by a fine rose window at the south end with glass by Evie Hone (1953). Some of the richly adorned side-chapels were added later by Henry Clutton, A. E. Purdie and Romaine-Walker.

ABOVE Church of the Immaculate Conception;
ABOVE RIGHT Notre Dame de France; LEFT Holy Trinity,
Marylebone; ABOVE LEFT Grosvenor Chapel

NOTRE DAME DE FRANCE Leicester Square, WC2
(Hector O. Corfiato, 1953-5)

The Roman Catholic Church of Notre Dame de France stands on the site of a former nineteenth-century church which had been converted by Louis-Auguste Boileau from a panorama, built in 1791 by Robert Barker. Boileau's highly original design, which had used the circumference of the panorama in combination with unconcealed iron piers, iron arches and iron ribs, was irretrievably damaged in 1940. The present building, designed by Professor Hector Corfiato in a style known as Beaux Arts Modern and built between 1953–5, is also circular in shape and rests on giant rounded piers. The façade is built of narrow bricks, the upper storeys reminiscent of a block of flats. The lower front is concave, with reliefs on either side of the main entrance. A glass and concrete lantern rises above a flat glass ceiling.

The interior displays over the high altar a tapestry woven at Aubusson and designed by Dom Robert of Buckfast. The mosaics of the side altar are by Boris Anrep, and the 1960 wall paintings in the Lady Chapel which depict the Annunciation, the Crucifixion and the Assumption are by Jean Cocteau.

◆

CHURCH OF OUR LADY OF THE ASSUMPTION AND ST GREGORY
Warwick Street, W1 (1788)

Originally the chapel of the Portuguese Embassy, Our Lady of the Assumption was transferred to the Bavarian Embassy in 1736. The chapel was destroyed in the Gordon Riots and rebuilt in 1788. The present building is in homely red brick with three blank arches on the street front, emphasised by a large pediment. Inside, on columns painted to look like wood, there are three galleries to which a cast-iron balustrade was added by J. F. Bentley in the 1870s. At the same time, he imparted a new look to the east end with marble panels and mosaics. The statue, known as Our Lady of Warwick Street, was erected in 1875. Bentley's work was not completed until well into this century. The marble altar is Italian dating from the early nineteenth century; the font is about 1788. The large relief of the Assumption is by J. E. Carew, 1853.

◆

THE QUEEN'S CHAPEL
Marlborough Road, SW1
(Inigo Jones, 1623-7)

The Queen's Chapel, one of the few authentic works still remaining by Inigo Jones, was started in 1623 for the Infanta of Spain, intended bride of Charles I, and completed in 1627 for Henrietta Maria, the French princess he did marry. Despoiled during the Commonwealth, it was refurbished in 1662 for Catherine of Braganza, Portuguese wife of Charles II, and since then has served many Queens of differing nationalities. Roman Catholic, Dutch Reformed and Danish services have all been held here, and it was here that George III married Princess Charlotte of Mecklenburg-Strelitz in 1761. From the eighteenth century until 1901 it was known as the German Chapel Royal.

The exterior, which is rendered to look like ashlar, has Portland stone dressings, and is pedimented at either end. Below the eastern pediment there is a huge Venetian window, generally supposed to be the first of its kind in England. The chapel is entered beneath a deep gallery, and the simple interior has a wooden coffered vault, decorated in gold and white with a detailed cornice beneath. Most of the furnishings are late seventeenth century, including the greyish-green panelling of the lower walls, although the magnificent chimneypiece in the west gallery, which used to be the Royal Pew, is by Inigo Jones himself.

The Chapel is open for Sunday Services in summer except in August and September.

◆

LEFT Church of our Lady of the Assumption and St Gregory

RIGHT The Queen's Chapel

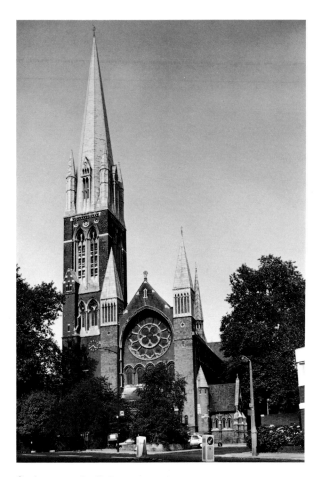

St Augustine's, Kilburn

ST AUGUSTINE'S, KILBURN
Kilburn Park Road, NW6
(J. L. Pearson, 1871-98)

St Augustine's is universally acclaimed as a superb church, and its design was to form the prototype for many of J. L. Pearson's later churches. It was built to serve the High Church faction of St Mary's, Kilburn, who abandoned their Low Church parish to found a new place of worship under the leadership of their Tractarian curate, the Rev. Richard Carr Kirkpatrick. Pearson's avowed intention was to 'bring people soonest to their knees', and the church he created here expresses a spiritual conviction that is deeply satisfying.

The exterior has a spectacular west front in which a dominant rose window, framed by tall narrow turrets, is joined to a Gothic steeple, soaring 254 feet high, all in the manner of the thirteenth century, with an abundance of lancet windows. The red brick interior is an original and arresting composition of galleries, columns and internal buttresses, rib-vaulted throughout, which produces a wonderful sense of space and

harmony. There is a plentiful use of stone in the chancel, which is separated from the nave by a screen of five arches, carrying a broad band of carving surmounted by the Cross which is flanked by stone figures from the Passion. Furnishings and decoration are in the High Victorian manner with inlaid marble, much ornate carving and wall paintings executed by Clayton and Bell, who also designed all the glass.

Sir John Betjeman greatly admired this church, and claimed that the best way to see it was to walk right round the interior watching the constantly changing vista. And certainly, as an architectural affirmation of religious faith, the Church of St Augustine is well worth looking at.

◆

ST BARNABAS'S, PIMLICO
St Barnabas Street, Pimlico Road, SW1
(Thomas Cundy, 1847-50)

St Barnabas's was founded by the Reverend W. J. E. Bennett in the slum area of Pimlico, which formed part of his parish of St Paul's, Wilton Place, Knightsbridge. Complete with clergyhouse and school, it was built by Thomas Cundy in the Early English lancet style and is constructed in rough pale ragstone. The church has a nave and chancel with aisles, a tower and spire at the north-west and a south porch. The *Ecclesiologist*, while finding some design faults, conceded that it was 'the most complete and sumptuous church dedicated since the revival'.

The foundation stone had been laid by Dr Pusey in 1847 and the church was consecrated in 1850, but from the start there was conflict over its High Church ritual. This, in truth, was moderate enough; nevertheless, the twice-daily choral services, seasonal changes of altar frontals and lighted candles soon gave rise to the nickname 'Convent of the Belgravians'. The Low Church faction was incensed and in 1850–51, during a general anti-Papacy scare, St Barnabas's became a focus of rioting. In a speech that did nothing to soothe the situation, Lord Shaftesbury proclaimed that he 'would rather worship with Lydia on the banks of the river than with a hundred surpliced priests in the gorgeous temple of St Barnabas' (Acts xvi). The term 'Lydian worship' became an ecclesiastical catchphrase, and Canon Clarke recounts the amusement felt when someone remembered an early novel, *The Nun of Arrouca*, by Lord John Russell, in which the hero, having abducted a novice from a convent in Portugal, sits beside her close to a river: 'Catherine leaned towards him, her soul seemed to melt at his voice; by an impulse of the moment he moved towards her, and their lips met.' Now, said the *Ecclesiologist* with delight, we know what 'Lydian worship' really means!

Later additions and adornments to the church include a reredos and decorative paintings by Bodley and Garner (1893), the Lady Chapel by Sir Ninian Comper (1900), and a new east window (1953), also by Comper.

◆

ST CLEMENT DANES
Strand, WC2
(Christopher Wren, 1680-2;
Steeple, James Gibbs, 1719)

The early connection with the Danes is obscure. According to John Stow it was 'because Harold [Harefoot], a Danish King and other Danes were buried here'. Another supposition is that Danes married to English women were allowed by Alfred the Great to live between Westminster and Ludgate where, in the words of William Fleetwood, Recorder of London in 1581, 'they builded a synagogue, the which being afterwards consecrated, was called Ecclesia Clemtis Danorum'.

St Clement's survived the Great Fire, but shortly afterwards became so decayed that rebuilding was essential. The new church, by Christopher Wren, is the only one of his churches (except for St Paul's) to have an apse. He kept the old tower, refacing it with stone and disguising the buttresses as attached obelisks. The vestries on either side are domed, and the graceful three-stage steeple was added in 1719 by James Gibbs.

The church was gutted in 1941 by a bomb which left the walls and steeple standing. With contributions from the Royal Air Force and from Commonwealth and Allied Air Forces it was extremely well restored by W. A. S. Lloyd. He renewed the rich decoration and ornate plasterwork, originally created by Edward Pearce and John Shorthose, and repaired the fine woodwork. The white walls, brilliantly lit by the windows

St Clement Danes

of clear, slightly rippled glass, set off the dark woodwork and white columns. The pulpit is an original furnishing which was stored in St Paul's during the war. The fine reredos above the altar, painted in gold, depicts the Annunciation and is by Ruskin Spear. An early adornment, lost during the war, was a picture of Saint Cecilia which used to hang over the altar. It had caused a furore in 1725 when it was alleged that an angel, 'supposed to be beating time to the Musick', was a portrait of Princess Sobieski, wife of the Pretender. 'The tinctured Abomination' was consequently removed by the Bishop of London and returned to St Clement's only in 1900. The west end is dominated by the splendid organ, gift in 1956 of the United States Air Force and families, designed by Ralph Downes and made by Harrison & Harrison of Durham in a case based on Father Smith's of 1690. The ancient crypt has been converted into a chapel, the chains inside the door being a relic of the time when coffins had to be secured from body snatchers.

In the eighteenth century Samuel Johnson was a regular worshipper, occupying seat no. 18 in the north gallery. His attendance is commemorated by a brass plaque on a nearby pillar and a statue of him stands outside. In 1784, in a letter to his friend Mrs Thrale, Johnson wrote: 'After a confinement of 129 days, more than the third part of a year, and no inconsiderable part of human life, I returned this day thanks to God in St Clement's Church for my recovery.' The new peal of ten bells, hung in 1957, frequently rings out the tune of the nursery rhyme *Oranges and Lemons*. The verses, when sung in full, are intended to imitate the sounds of the old London church bells. However, the St Clements referred to in the rhyme is probably St Clement's, Eastcheap, which stands near the wharves where citrus fruit from the Mediterranean used to be unloaded.

Mementos connected with the Royal Air Force are all around. Over 750 Air Force badges cut from Welsh slate are displayed in the floor and there is a complete roll of all who died in action. The names of 19,000 American airmen, based here during the war, are also commemorated in a special shrine. St Clement Danes is the headquarters church of the Royal Air Force. The Air Council has its own pews, and ceremonial services are held here.

◆

LEFT St Clement Danes

ST CYPRIAN'S, CLARENCE GATE
Glentworth Street, Marylebone, NW1
(William Bucknall and Ninian Comper, 1903)

At its consecration, the floor of St Cyprian's was strewn with flowers and rushes in a display of refined medievalism considered a fitting accompaniment to what Sir Ninian Comper described as 'the last development of a purely English parish church'. It was built as a memorial to the Rev. Charles Gutch who, until his death in 1896, had laboured for thirty years, single-mindedly devoted to the relief of the poor and sick in the parish. His ministry had been obstructed by Lord Portman's refusal to let him build his own church, Portman disapproving of Gutch's liturgical practice, and he had to make shift, without assurance of residence or stipend, in an improvised place of worship adapted for him out of two houses and a coalshed by G. E. Street. Only after his death was a site at last made available for the church he had wanted so much.

The exterior of St Cyprian's is in brick, completely plain without tower or turret. The interior is exuberantly spacious and light, with tall, slender

Rood screen detail, St Cyprian's, Clarence Gate

columns and stone arches, uncluttered by pews and showing a shining expanse of parquet floor. There are chapels on either side, the north one containing the altar formerly used by Gutch. All the furnishings, including the rood screen, lacy and gilded, the tall gilt classical font cover and the stained glass were designed by Comper himself.

◆

ST GEORGE'S, HANOVER SQUARE
St George Street, Hanover Square, W1
(John James, 1712-24)

Although work on St George's began in 1712, the building was spread over twelve years. The new church was to serve an estate being developed north of Piccadilly, and, as one of the Fifty New Churches, was financed under the 1711 Act. The architect, John James, succeeded James Gibbs as one of the Commissioners of the Act in 1715. His church is in the grand manner, solid and stone-faced, the front dominated by a huge Corinthian portico which, the first of its kind in London, just preceded Hawksmoor's St George's, Bloomsbury and Gibbs's St Martin-in-the-Fields. Behind and above it rises a bell-tower, and the north side shows two tiers of windows linked together by heavy rustication. The interior offers no surprises. It is large and dignified with north and south galleries, and a ceiling featuring square gilded panels. The altarpiece contains a darkened paint-ing of the Last Supper by James Thornhill; above it, in brilliant contrast, is a display of dazzling sixteenth-century Flemish glass brought over in the 1840s and adapted to fit the Venetian window it adorns. The organ, originally built by Gerard Smith, nephew of the renowned Father Smith, has been rebuilt most recently by Harrison & Harrison of Durham. In its heyday it must often have been heard by Handel, who lived for thirty-four years in nearby Brook Street and regularly worshipped here.

In 1762, the church received a visit from James Boswell who heard a good sermon but was rather inattentive as the Duchess of Grafton 'attracted his eyes too much'. St George's has always been the church for fashionable weddings; Lady Ham-ilton in 1791; Shelley in 1814; Disraeli in 1839; Lord Asquith in 1894.

The two cast-iron dogs in the porch, formerly outside a shop in Conduit Street, are by Adrian Jones.

ST JAMES THE LESS
Thorndike Street, SW1
(G. E. Street, 1860-61)

This, the first church designed in London by G. E. Street, was built at the expense of three sisters, the Misses Monk, in memory of their father, the Bishop of Gloucester. The unusual form of its Gothic design caused contemporary critics to protest at its 'foreignness', but later opinion has approved of its vigour and originality. Solidly built in red and black brick, the body of the church is all but completely detached from the tower. The theme of red and black is repeated in the interior which consists of three wide bays and a clerestory.

ABOVE St James the Less

LEFT St George's, Hanover Square

The arcades are in notched polychromatic brick. The chancel is distinctly separate from the nave, the division emphasised by the chancel arch above a fine early fresco by G. F. Watts.

When St James's was completed, the *Illustrated London News*, comparing its pristine newness with the poor neighbourhood around it, remarked that it rose 'as a lily among weeds'. Grouped with the parish hall and school and surrounded by mag-

St James the Less

nificent wrought-iron railings, the church now forms the centre of the 1960s Lillington Gardens Estate.

◆

ST JAMES'S, PICCADILLY
Piccadilly, W1
(Christopher Wren, 1676-84)

At his Restoration King Charles II granted to his loyal courtier, Henry Jermyn, Earl of St Albans, the leasehold of land in Westminster which had belonged to St James's Palace and was known as St James's Fields. The Earl developed the area and commissioned Christopher Wren to build a church which would serve the new parish.

St James's, consecrated in 1684, is particularly interesting as it was the only church in London to be built by Wren upon a virgin site, and, incorporating his ideal of a parish church, it served as a prototype for many of the urban churches built during the eighteenth century. These concepts are embodied in a much-quoted letter written by Wren in 1708 when he was appointed a Commissioner for the Fifty New Churches:

The Romanists, indeed, may build larger Churches, it is enough if they hear the Murmur of the Mass, and see the Elevation of the Host, but ours are to be fitted with Auditories. I can hardly think it practicable to make a single Room so capacious, with Pews and Galleries, as to hold above 2,000 Persons, and all to hear the Service, and both to hear distinctly, and see the Preacher. I endeavoured to effect this, in building the Parish Church of St James's, Westminster, which, I presume, is the most capacious, with the Qualifications, that hath yet been built ... In this Church I mention, though very broad, and the middle Nave arched up, yet as there are no Walls of a second Order, nor Lanterns, nor Buttresses, but the whole Roof rests upon the Pillars, as do also the Galleries; I think it may be found beautiful and convenient, and as such, the cheapest of any Form I could invent.

The church is constructed in plain brick with Portland stone dressings and round-headed windows. A domed top had been planned by Wren but was rejected, and the spire chosen to mount the balustraded tower was actually designed by Edward Willcox and erected in 1699. It was replaced by a replica in fibreglass in a post-Second

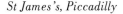

St James's, Piccadilly

St James's, Spanish Place

World War restoration carried out by Sir Albert Richardson. An unusual feature of the exterior is a pulpit, installed on the north wall in 1902, but unused since the advent of modern traffic.

The first impression on entering the church is one of light, which streams in through the large clear windows, illuminating the elegant proportions of the interior and enhancing the beautiful plaster work. The furnishings are handsome and include three notable pieces by Grinling Gibbons which were saved from destruction during the war by being stored at Hardwick Hall in Derbyshire. These are, the font in white marble which features the Tree of Life (see picture page 99); the reredos, so beautifully carved that John Evelyn, after a visit to 'the new church at St James's, elegantly built' in 1684, wrote, 'There was no altar anywhere in England, nor has there been any abroad, more handsomely adorned'; and the case containing the Renatus Harris organ. This exceptionally fine instrument, which was originally built for James II in 1684 for his chapel at Whitehall, was given to St James's, Piccadilly by Queen Mary in 1691.

There are many monuments to prominent figures of the past, both literary and artistic, including the Dutch marine painters Van de Velde, father and son; James Gillray, the caricaturist; and James Dodley, brother and partner of Dr Johnson's publisher, who is commemorated by the sculptor, John Flaxman. In this church, William Pitt the Younger, and William Blake, poet and painter, were baptised; and here, in 1865, Sir Samuel Baker, the explorer, was discreetly married to his mistress, a young Hungarian whom he had bought at a slave auction in a Turkish bazaar.

St James's is frequently the venue for concerts, exhibitions and talks by visiting guest preachers and lecturers. Formerly approached from Jermyn Street, the church's main entrance is now from Piccadilly and is flanked by a Garden of Remembrance.

◆

ST JAMES'S, SPANISH PLACE
Spanish Place, George Street, W1
(Edward Goldie, 1885-90)

St James's was built in the late 1880s to replace a chapel, by Joseph Bonomi, which had been attached to the Spanish Embassy. The present Roman Catholic church, designed by Edward Goldie, is Early English in style and constructed of Kentish ragstone. It is very large, and faces west, with nave, aisles and narrow outer aisles. The confessionals are concealed as part of a wall arcade and the transepts are spanned by a great gallery.

Most of the furnishings are by J. F. Bentley, but the reredos and hanging *baldacchino* are by Thomas Garner. The alabaster Stations of the Cross and the baptistry gates, all added in 1915, are the work of Geoffrey Webb.

◆

ST JAMES'S, SUSSEX GARDENS, W2
(John Goldicutt and George Gutch, 1841-3; G. E. Street, 1881)

The first church of St James was built between 1841–3 to ease the pressure on St Mary, Paddington Green, whose parish had greatly increased. The architects were Goldicutt and Gutch and their church was in yellow brick. By 1881, the need for a bigger church was imperative, and the designs for its enlargement were carried out by G. E. Street. His plan was ingenious. Retaining the tower and porches of the original building, he turned the church round, ignoring the orthodox orientation, and placed the chancel at the west end. The outside he faced with flint, and the prevailing style throughout is Perpendicular. Street died in 1881 before the work was finished, and the church was completed by Sir Arthur Blomfield.

◆

ST JOHN'S, SMITH SQUARE, SW1
(Thomas Archer, 1714-28)

Built between 1714–28 by Thomas Archer, St John's was one of the Fifty New Churches. It is a huge, handsome edifice, solid and much pedimented. The four tall, pierced towers, inspired by Borromini and finished with lead cupolas and pineapples, have been frequently derided by Classical purists. Indeed, in the nineteenth century the church was far from admired and Charles Dickens was reflecting Victorian opinion when, in *Our Mutual Friend*, he described it as 'a very hideous church with four towers at the corners, generally resembling some petrified monster, frightful and gigantic, on its back with its legs in the air'.

Almost since its completion, St John's has been dogged by misfortune. In 1742, it was gutted by fire and was rebuilt without the twelve Corinthian columns which had formed an atrium and supported the ceiling; in 1812 it was given rough timber props, which were removed in 1824 by Inwood during a general refurbishment in the Grecian style. In 1941 the church was again burned out and remained for more than twenty years a ruin while proposals for its future were discussed and rejected. But eventually, after a restoration by Marshall Sisson who returned as nearly as possible to its original appearance, St John's was reopened in 1968 as a concert hall, complete with Corinthian columns and atrium and with excellent acoustics.

RIGHT Font by Grinling Gibbons, St James's, Piccadilly

LEFT St James's, Sussex Gardens

ST JOHN'S WOOD CHURCH
St John's Wood High Street, NW8
(Thomas Hardwick, 1813-14)

This pretty little church was designed by Thomas Hardwick as a chapel of ease for the parish church of St Marylebone to serve the new suburb of St John's Wood, once an area owned by the Priory of St John's, Clerkenwell. The church was made parochial in 1952. The west front has an Ionic portico, pediment and turret all faced in stone, the sides showing exposed brick. Inside, the gallery, resting on Tuscan pillars, which originally extended all round the church, was enclosed by glass above the nave on either side during the 1920s, leaving only the west gallery as an integral part of the charming interior. There had been alterations in Victorian times, but a post-war restoration has renewed its Georgian appearance and replaced the former box pews. These are now painted white to match the white and gold decoration.

Among those buried in the churchyard was Joanna Southcott (died 1814), a religious fanatic so notorious in her day that, to avoid scandal, she was interred under the assumed name of Goddard. Subsequently two memorials were erected to her.

◆

ST MARGARET'S, WESTMINSTER
Parliament Square, SW1 (1523)

St Margaret's was founded in the eleventh or early twelfth century on a site adjacent to Westminster Abbey, under whose jurisdiction it stayed until 1840 when it came under the episcopal hierarchy. The present church derives from the early sixteenth century although only the arcades and the arch of the tower actually date from then. Not many years after it had been completed, it was threatened with demolition by the Lord Protector to provide stone for the building of Somerset House, and only armed resistance by the resentful parishioners kept it intact.

In 1614 it was adopted as the parish church of the House of Commons, and it was here in 1642 that members took the Solemn League and Covenant against Popery. John Pym died the following year, and in 1661 his body and those of other Parliamentarians buried in Westminster Abbey were disinterred and all thrown into a pit in the churchyard of St Margaret's. No thought of this was in Samuel Pepys's mind when, six years later, he attended a service here and amused himself, 'with my perspective glass up and down the church, by which I had the pleasure of seeing and gazing at a great many fine women, and what with that, and sleeping, I passed away the time till sermon was done'.

In the centuries that followed, many alterations and restorations have taken place, with the east end being several times rebuilt, the last time in 1905 when the magnificent east window was reset. This contains rare Flemish glass of great beauty which is said to have been the gift of King Ferdinand and his Queen to celebrate the betrothal of their daughter, Katharine of Aragon, to Prince Arthur, eldest son of Henry VII. After Arthur's death, the glass passed into private hands until in 1758 it was bought for £420 and instated here.

St Margaret's makes a charming picture, clad

ABOVE LEFT St John's, Smith Square

RIGHT St John's Wood Church

St Margaret's, Westminster

ST MARK'S, HAMILTON TERRACE
Hamilton Terrace, NW8 (Thomas Cundy and Thomas Cundy the Younger, 1846-7)

St Mark's, built in 1846–7 by the Cundys, father and son, is large and Perpendicular, 'a very neat specimen of modern church building in the Early English style of architecture', according to the *Illustrated London News* of July 1847. The same article described the interior as 'very spacious, and from there being no arches to divide it into nave and aisle, the span of the open timber roof is very great'. In the opinion of the twentieth-century critic, H. S. Goodhart-Rendel, however, its appearance invites comparison with a 'large broad Gothic riding school'.

It is galleried on three sides; the ceiling above the sanctuary is painted with angels and florets, and the glass is by Clayton and Bell. The chancel, designed by E. B. Ferrey, was added in 1877–8 by the vicar, Canon Duckworth, a close friend of Lewis Carroll. The church was damaged during the Second World War but was afterwards restored, the spire being rebuilt in 1955.

◆

ST MARTIN-IN-THE-FIELDS
Trafalgar Square, WC2 (James Gibbs, 1721-6)

The medieval chapel which stood on this site was surrounded by fields belonging to Westminster Abbey, hence its name. First mentioned in 1222, it did not receive parochial status until the reign of Henry VIII, probably to enable victims of the plague to be buried here rather than be transported via the royal Palace of Westminster to St Margaret's. Two years later, in 1544, the chapel was rebuilt and gradually it became adopted as the church of the royal parish.

By 1721, the Tudor building was too small for the greatly increased congregation, and James Gibbs was commissioned to design a new church. His first plan for a circular structure was rejected, but his alternative design of a temple front, complete with a pedimented portico on vast columns, the whole straddled by a magnificent steeple – a dramatic combination which was later widely copied – found favour. The new church was consecrated in 1726 and must have looked out of place in its original modest setting. However, a hundred

in stone and framed by a level lawn, its tower standing high above the low roofed nave. Entrance from the west is through a nineteenth-century porch. The plan inside is the usual late Perpendicular rectangle with no division between nave and chancel, allowing an unimpeded view of the brilliant colours of the east window. The arcades are of eight bays, and the side aisles are full of interesting monuments. The south aisle windows are of an abstract design by John Piper.

Among the many notable dead buried here is Sir Walter Raleigh, whose headless body lies before the altar. His head is far away in West Horsley. From 1676 until his death in 1708 Father Smith was organist here. Today's instrument, however, is a Walker which was installed in 1897 and has since been completely rebuilt. The theme of music is a constant one, and the church is in regular use for recitals and concerts. Another theme is weddings: Samuel Pepys was married here in 1655; so was John Milton, to his second wife, in 1656; and Winston Churchill in 1908.

A photograph of St Margaret's appears on page 11.

years later it was given a spectacular prominence, in keeping with its grandiose appearance, by the formation of Trafalgar Square.

Its interior is reminiscent of Wren's design of St James's, Piccadilly. A tunnel-vault, rising above arches carried on tall columns, with galleries on three sides, overhangs an unusually wide nave. This ends with quadrant walls curving into a narrow chancel with panelled rooms above (originally royal pews) which open into the church as well as into the chancel. The effect is striking, and combined with the beautiful plasterwork of Artari and Bagutti impressed one early critic as 'a little too gay and theatrical for Protestant worship'. The oval font with its finely carved cover is from the earlier church and dates from 1689. The choir stalls and the pulpit were installed in 1799, as were the box pews in the aisles which were lowered in 1858. The church is beautifully light, dominated by a huge Venetian window of plain glass with a central blue cross, instated after the war.

As well as many links with royalty – Charles II was baptised here in 1630, Mary II attended

St Martin-in-the-Fields

services, and George I was the first churchwarden of the present church – St Martin's has been associated with a large number of distinguished people, many of whom were buried here. These include the miniaturist, Nicholas Hilliard in 1619; Nell Gwynne in 1687; John Hampden in 1696; the highwayman, Jack Sheppard in 1742; and the painters, William Hogarth in 1764 and Sir Joshua Reynolds in 1792.

In this century, through the inspired and compassionate ministry of H. R. L. (Dick) Sheppard and his successors, St Martin's has become a byword for charity. The crypt, which was for many years open to the homeless, now offers sustenance to the hungry on Sunday mornings and on Christmas Day. Unlike the vast majority of London churches, St Martin's stays open until 9 p.m. There are frequent midday concerts. Such is the reputation of this much loved church that a letter, addressed in 1983 to 'God, somewhere in London', was delivered to St Martin's.

◆

ST MARY-LE-STRAND
Strand, WC2 (James Gibbs, 1714-17)

First mentioned in 1147 and known as the Church of the Nativity of Our Lady and the Innocents, St Mary's was demolished in 1549 to make way for Somerset House. The Lord Protector had pledged himself to rebuild the church, but he failed to keep his promise and for nearly 200 years the parishioners were obliged to worship in the Savoy Chapel. Early in the eighteenth century, however, their parish became eligible for a new church under the 1711 Act, and St Mary's was the first of the fifty to be built.

The architect was James Gibbs, and the site a narrow island in the middle of the Strand. His church is an elegant one, built in stone, the detail throughout showing a strong Roman influence, a legacy of his early training under Carlo Fontana. In his own words, 'it consists of two orders, in the upper of which lights are placed: the wall of the lower, being solid to keep out the noises from the street, is adorned with niches'. The church is entered by an Italianate semi-circular portico on the west front. The stage above carries a large central pediment behind which the tower rises directly in three stages. There was to have been a bell-turret, and the tower was added only after a plan to mount a statue of Queen Anne on a column in the foreground was abandoned. The theme of two orders is repeated inside, with rich architectural detail around the high windows and ceiling. There are no aisles, just a projecting apse, framed by twin Corinthian columns and decorated

The pulpit, St Mary-le-Strand

with cherubs' heads and the like. By the late 1970s the church was in dire need of restoration and an appeal was launched to rescue it. Today, renewed and whole, it makes a charming setting for the exhibitions and concerts held in it.

◆

ST MARY'S, PADDINGTON
Paddington Green, W2
(John Plaw, 1788-91)

The ancient parish church of St Mary, founded in the thirteenth century to serve the little village of Paddington, was demolished in 1678 and replaced

by one that had a bell-turret at the west end crowned by a small spire. From this spire bread used to be thrown, in a strange annual custom, for people to scramble for below. The second church gave way, in 1788, to the present one, designed by John Plaw. It was consecrated in 1791 and remained parochial until 1845, when the parish was transferred to the new and more spacious St James's, Sussex Gardens.

Plaw's church is a modest little square in stock brick, conceived on the Greek cross plan with three porticos topped with a white cupola. The concessionary strip of green on which it still stands is hemmed in by the motorway which runs alongside. Nineteenth-century alterations had changed the character of the interior, but an exemplary restoration in the 1970s by Raymond Erith has renewed all its late eighteenth-century charm. In the central square three-sided galleries recede into the arms of the cross making up nine sides of a dodecagon. The galleries rest on columns, those at the angles being stouter to support the four upper columns which carry the shallow dome. The delicacy of the architecture, with its display of segmental vaults and arches, is enhanced by the furnishings, both old and new, which include a set of box pews, the original font, pulpit and altar and a fine chandelier designed by Erith himself.

John Donne preached his first sermon in the original parish church; and Sarah Siddons, whose death in 1831 is commemorated by a tablet in the church, is buried in the churchyard. There is a statue to her on the Green. William Hogarth was married in the old church in 1730.

In addition to regular worship, St Mary's is used for concerts.

◆

ST MARY MAGDALENE, PADDINGTON
Woodchester Square, W2
(G. E. Street, 1868-78)

St Mary's was built at the instigation of R. T. West, curate of All Saints, Margaret Street, who wanted to provide similar High Church services for the poor people of Paddington. Street, a member of the congregation of All Saints, designed the church on a peculiarly difficult site.

RIGHT St Mary-le-Strand

The angels between the windows of the arcade in the richly decorated interior are by Thomas Earp. The gorgeous chapel in the crypt is an early work by Ninian Comper (1895).

◆

ST MARYLEBONE
Marylebone Road (opposite York Gate), W1
(Thomas Hardwick the Younger, 1813-17)

The first little parish church, built in about 1200 on a site in what is now Oxford Street, was dedicated to St John. A second church, built in about 1400 close to the present site, became known as St Mary at Bourne, in allusion to the nearby River Tyburn formerly called the River Bourne. This was replaced in 1740 by a third church, which was soon found to be inadequate, and during the 1770s Sir William Chambers drew up several sets of plans for yet another building. These were all rejected by the vestry, and so too were proposals for a new parish church to be built at the southern end of Portland Place as part of John Nash's scheme for Regent's Park. However, when the Duke of

Portland threatened to close up Portland Place unless the church was built on his land, Thomas Hardwick was commissioned by the vestry to make the plans for a fourth church, which was built between 1813–17 on the present site in a style inspired by one of Chambers' rejected designs. In its early stages the building was intended to be a chapel of ease; but, when it was half-completed, the vestry decided to make it the parish church and demote the old St Marylebone to parish chapel, which it remained until its demolition in 1949.

The magnificent Corinthian portico of the present parish church faces north to York Gate in an arrangement specially contrived by John Nash in his layout of Regent's Park. The tower rising behind the portico carries a circle of free-standing columns topped by a stone cupola with a clasping of caryatids. Flanking the window at the east end are two diagonal, projecting wings built for purposes which have remained obscure. The interior underwent an overall Victorian trans-

LEFT St Marylebone

BELOW St Mary's, Paddington

formation in 1883 when Thomas Harris, church-warden, remodelled the choir, removed galleries, put in stalls and built an apse; and it now bears little resemblance to the original design.

Numerous celebrated people have been baptised, married or buried in St Marylebone's Church. Lord Byron was christened here in 1788; James Gibbs (died 1754), George Stubbs (died 1806) and James Northcote (died 1831) all lie in the former churchyard, which is now a 'garden of rest' in Marylebone High Street.

In the second church of St Marylebone, Francis Bacon married Alice Barnham in 1606. It also formed the scene of the marriage of the Rake in plate V of Hogarth's 'Rake's Progress'. In the third church, Richard Brinsley Sheridan married Elizabeth Linley in 1773; and in the present church Elizabeth Barrett married Robert Browning in a secret ceremony in 1846. There is a memorial room to them in the church. St Marylebone is described by Charles Dickens in *Dombey and Son* and is probably the setting for Mr Dombey's marriage to Edith Granger.

ST PATRICK'S
Soho Square, W1 (John Kelly, 1891-3)

An eighteenth-century church manuscript records that in 1791, 'a very numerous and respectable body of Catholics conceived the wise and charitable project of establishing a Catholic Chapel' in the neighbourhood of St Giles, then largely inhabited by poor Irish immigrants. The chapel was built in 1792 and was dedicated to St Patrick. A hundred years later it was demolished to make way for the present church. This was designed by John Kelly and completed in 1893. It is of red brick in a simplified Renaissance style, fronted by a campanile with a doorway to the square. Entrance is through an ante-room. The interior is impressive with shallow side chapels instead of aisles. The general feeling is very Italian.

◆

ST PAUL'S, COVENT GARDEN
Covent Garden, WC2
(Inigo Jones, 1633; rebuilt,
Thomas Hardwick the Younger, 1796)

In the Middle Ages Covent Garden was known as 'the Garden of the Convent', and produced vegetables for Westminster Abbey. The site, granted by the Crown in 1553 to Sir John Russell, was developed by his descendant, the 4th Earl of Bedford, in the early seventeenth century. Inigo Jones was commissioned to lay out an imposing piazza, the focus of which was to be the church. According to an often-quoted account by Horace Walpole, the Earl, anxious to keep down the cost, declared he would not have the church much better than a barn. Jones's reply – 'Well then, you shall have the handsomest barn in England' – has passed into the annals of history. St Paul's was built in 1633, consecrated as a chapel of ease to St Martin-in-the-Fields in 1638, and became a parish church in 1645. There have been structural changes since it was built, but the design remains very simple with brick walls, chalet roof and a huge Tuscan portico at the east end. The wings which used to flank it on either side, together with the former cupolas on the roof, disappeared long ago. Nevertheless, successive restorations and adjustments have not significantly altered its general appearance.

There are no aisles to the interior; the ceiling,

originally painted by Matthew Goodrich, is now plain; and the altar is enclosed with columns taken from the side galleries when these were removed in 1872.

St Paul's is rich in theatrical associations. It was here (or perhaps in the piazza) that on 9 May 1662, Samuel Pepys watched the antics of 'an Italian puppet play' which was 'very pretty'; and more recently, the portico has provided the setting for the opening scene of Bernard Shaw's *Pygmalion*. Scores of theatre people are commemorated here: the plaques on the wall almost constitute a theatrical *Who's Who*. Amongst those buried here were Sir Peter Lely (1680), William Wycherley (1715), Grinling Gibbons (1721), Thomas Arne (1778), Thomas Rowlandson (1827), and among them may also lie the body of the highwayman, Claude Duval, who was hanged at Tyburn in 1670, and who is commemorated by these words:

> *Here lies Duvall; Reader if male thou art*
> *Look to thy purse; if female to thy heart.*

St Paul's remains today the spiritual centre of the theatre world, and is the headquarters of the Actors' Church Union.

ABOVE St Paul's, Covent Garden

LEFT St Patrick's, Soho Square

ST PAUL'S, KNIGHTSBRIDGE
Wilton Place, SW1
(Thomas Cundy, 1840-3)

St Paul's was one of several churches built to serve the newly developed Grosvenor Estate. It was designed in the Perpendicular style by Thomas Cundy and was the subject of considerable alteration towards the end of the century. It is very large, in yellow brick with lancet windows filled with tracery. The west tower was formerly topped by pinnacles, which gave way to a parapet built later by G. F. Bodley. There is a fine east window of 1892, the work of Lavers and Westlake, who also made the windows of the south chapel in 1895.

The church's early history was marked by strife. The first vicar, W. J. E. Bennett, left in 1851 to go to Frome, unable any longer to endure the strictures of Bishop Blomfield upon his High

Church practices. After his departure, the candles, credence and surpliced choir vanished, but eventually came back again.

◆

SAVOY CHAPEL
The Queen's Chapel of the Savoy, Savoy Street, WC2 (Sydney Smirke, 1865)

The present chapel is a nineteenth-century reconstruction by Sydney Smirke of an early sixteenth-century building, the origins of which were earlier still. Its sad appearance today, hemmed in by vast hotels and offices, belies its interesting history.

In 1246 Henry III gave a piece of land bordering the Thames to his wife's uncle, Peter of Savoy, who built himself a manor there. After his death it changed hands several times, passing finally to John of Gaunt in whose ownership it was laid waste during the Peasants' Revolt of 1381. The site remained derelict until the beginning of the sixteenth century when Henry VII founded the Hospital of the Savoy which, completed in 1515, was furnished with a chapel dedicated to St John the Baptist. Later in the century, when the building of Somerset House deprived the parishioners

of St Mary-le-Strand of their church, they came here to worship and stayed until 1723. The Hospital was suppressed under Edward VI, revived by his sister, Mary Tudor, and finally dissolved in 1702, having for a long time provided the Master of the Savoy with a comfortable sinecure. The old Hospital buildings were not cleared away until the early nineteenth century, and in the interim several little foreign chapels (including a mosque) mushroomed in the precincts. Between 1728–56, the incumbent of the Savoy Chapel was John Wilkinson, who became notorious for his celebration of illegal marriages – 1,190 of them in 1755. Even early in this century, the chapel was well known for allowing remarriage of divorced persons. In 1773 it came under the direct jurisdiction of the Sovereign, a privilege which it still enjoys. Nearly ninety years later, it was gutted by fire and was rebuilt by Sydney Smirke in 1865. In 1957–8 there was an addition of an antechapel on the east side, designed by A. B. Knapp-Fisher.

The interior is without aisles, the roof a copy

LEFT St Paul's, Knightsbridge

BELOW Savoy Chapel

of the magnificent Tudor original. The walls are panelled, and at the south end there are sixteen stalls for the Royal Victorian Order for which this has been the Chapel since 1937.

◆

Also of interest in Westminster are Holy Trinity, Prince Consort Road, SW7, one of G. F. Bodley's last works (1902–3); St Mary's, Bryanston Square, W1 (1821–4) designed by Sir Robert Smirke, whose tall pepperpot tower has 'nothing to say', in Sir John Summerson's words, 'and goes to enormous lengths to say it'; St Mark's, North Audley Street, W1 (1825–8) which was built by J. P.

Gandy-Deering as a chapel of ease to St George's, Hanover Square and which was drastically restored by Sir Arthur Blomfield and is now closed; St Matthew's, Great Peter Street, SW1 (1849–51) by Sir George Gilbert Scott with a Lady Chapel by Sir Ninian Comper (rebuilt after a fire in 1977 to a reduced design by Donald Buttress; the church was again damaged by fire in 1987); the big, Greek Revival St Peter's, Eaton Square, SW1 (1824–7) by Henry Hakewill with alterations by Sir Arthur Blomfield in the 1870s (badly damaged by fire in 1987); and St Stephen's, Rochester Row, financed by Baroness Burdett Coutts and built in Northumbrian sandstone in 1847–50, on a site chosen for her by Charles Dickens, by Benjamin Ferrey, a pupil of A.W. Pugin.

◆

NORTH LONDON

BARNET

The interior is disappointing: in red brick with a barrel-vaulted and domed ceiling it has a conventional, classical appearance which hardly matches the originality and grandeur of the outside. The murals and ceiling paintings were added between 1920–29 by Walter Starmer, who also designed the west window in which St Jude holds a cross in his right hand and a church in his left.

St Jude's stands opposite to the Free Church which, by the same architect, resembles it in design.

◆

ST MARY'S, FINCHLEY
Hendon Lane, N3

The church, first mentioned here in 1274, probably stood on the site of an even earlier building, though dedication to St Mary was not made until the mid-fourteenth century. The building has been added to and repaired over the centuries, the last time in 1953 when it was restored after bomb damage received during the Second World War. The tower, nave and north aisle (which incorporates some twelfth-century stone fragments) are medieval. One of the south aisles was built in 1872 and the other was added in 1932. There are some notable monuments, and a fine collection of brasses, now wall-mounted, which date from 1480. One of these contains an extract from the last will and testament of Thomas Sanny (1509), who left '40 shillings yearly for priests to sing for my soule ... while the world shall last'. An aumbry, now housed in the north wall, and a font bowl, discovered in the rectory grounds during the nineteenth century, are both Norman.

◆

ST JUDE ON THE HILL
Central Square, Hampstead Garden Suburb, NW11 (Sir Edwin Lutyens, 1909-10)

In 1907 Sir Edwin Lutyens was appointed architect for the public buildings of Central Square, the nub of the fashionable new Hampstead Garden Suburb, initiated by Canon Samuel Barnett and his wife, Dame Henrietta. The Church of St Jude, the focal point of the design, takes its name from St Jude's, Whitechapel of which the Canon had been Vicar.

The exterior is a striking composition showing a mixture of styles blended freely together: a Gothic spire mounted on a Byzantine tower soars to an enormous height, while the steeply pitched roof of the nave dips almost to the ground. The principal windows are overhung by pediments reminiscent of Dutch gables, while the dormer windows display a Baroque tendency.

ABOVE LEFT St Mary's, Finchley

RIGHT St Jude on the Hill

BRENT

◆

ST ANDREW'S, KINGSBURY
Old Church Lane, NW9
(Samuel Dawkes, 1845-7; re-erected 1933-4)

St Andrew's is remarkable in that it was originally
built on one site and now stands on another. It
was first erected in Wells Street, Marylebone by
Samuel Dawkes in a Perpendicular style which
was grudgingly conceded by the *Ecclesiologist* to
be 'good of its sort'. Even its critics, however, have
found no fault with the furnishings which, apart
from Butterfield's 1847 lectern, were added later:
G. E. Street designed the much admired reredos,
the chancel screen and font; the font cover, sedilia
and canopied arch in the sanctuary are by J. L.
Pearson; and William Burges designed the litany
desk. The stained glass is mostly by Clayton and
Bell. The great east window was designed by Pugin
and executed by Hardman.

Between 1862–85, during the incumbency of
the Rev. Benjamin Webb, St Andrew's became
celebrated as a model of High Anglican worship.
It was also renowned for its resident choir. But by
1932, with the depopulation of the neighbourhood,
this much-loved church had become redundant
and the decision was taken to re-erect it in Kingsbury next to the old church there, a tiny ancient
building which was subsequently made into a
museum. St Andrew's was taken down, every
stone numbered, and was rebuilt on the present
site under the direction of W. A. Forsyth.
Although some changes were inevitable, it is
remarkably faithful to its former self. The former
Bishop of London Arthur Foley Winnington
Ingram, who re-consecrated it in 1934, declared
that it had 'dropped from heaven into Kingsbury'.
Certainly it looks very much at home there.

◆

ST MARY'S, WILLESDEN
Neasden Lane, NW10

St Mary's was founded, possibly on the site of
a Saxon church, to serve the royal manors of
Willesden-cum-Neasden bestowed on the Dean
and Chapter of St Paul's Cathedral by King Athel-
stan after his victory over the Danes at the Battle
of Brunanburh in 937 AD. By the sixteenth
century, the church had become a focus for pilgrims attracted by a shrine containing a statue of
Our Lady of Willesden which was supposed to
possess miraculous powers. Known as the Black
Virgin of Willesden, the image was described in a
report made to Thomas Cromwell in 1535 as 'made
of woode in colour like ebon of ancient work-
manship, onli save the upper part is thoroughly
playted over with silver'. The Lord Chancellor
took swift action against such idolatry, and the
Black Virgin, together with statues of Our Lady
from Walsingham and Ipswich, was taken to
London and burned at Chelsea. From that time
until 1902, each vicar of Willesden had to pay a
fine of £13 at his induction and 26 shillings annually thereafter. A modern Black Virgin, by C.
Stern, was installed in the church in 1972.

The earliest part of St Mary's dates from the
thirteenth century with fifteenth- and sixteenth-
century additions. In 1872, in the second of two

St Andrew's, Kingsbury

St Mary's, Willesden

Victorian restorations, the north aisle and a new south porch were added. Among the furnishings is an ancient Purbeck marble font (still with its original lead lining) which dates from about 1150; a magnificent fourteenth-century door forms the inner door to the south porch; and a carved oak Reformation altar-table, used until 1964, now stands in the north aisle. Brasses include memorials to members of the Roberts family, who were squires of Willesden and lived at Neasden. There are carved wall monuments in the sanctuary to Richard and Margaret Paine by Cornelius Cure (1606) and to Sir John Franklyn by John Colt (1647). Charles Reade, author of *The Cloister and the Hearth*, was buried here in 1884.

CAMDEN

◆

ALL HALLOWS
Savernake Road, NW3
(James Brooks, 1892-1901)

All Hallows was consecrated in 1901, the year of its architect's death. The chancel was added twelve years later by Sir Giles Gilbert Scott. Sir Nikolaus Pevsner considered this church to be one of the noblest of its date in England, and Brooks's undoubted masterpiece. Built in ragstone with ashlar dressings, it has no tower but is tall and long with, on both sides, tall slim windows enclosed by massive buttresses, the upper parts of which rise to the projecting vault at a steep diagonal, the effect being particularly impressive to the north.

Inside, the aisles are the same height as the nave, and high round piers support the beginnings of vaulting ribs but the vault itself has never been built. The upper parts of the nave therefore are of exposed brick but the rest of the interior is constructed in Ancaster limestone. At the west end is a very large wheel window.

ALL SAINTS, CAMDEN TOWN
Camden Street, NW1 (William Inwood and Henry William Inwood, 1822-4)

All Saints was built between 1822–4 as one of three chapels of ease for the parish of St Pancras. It was designed by the Inwoods, father and son, who had just completed St Pancras New Church, and it has been held by some to be a more inspired building than the latter, at a quarter of the cost. An issue of the *Gentleman's Magazine* of 1824 praised it as 'neat and substantial', and described the interior as 'very neat approaching to elegance'. It is rectangular in brick with a stone façade. A slender circular tower rises behind a big semi-circular portico of large fluted Ionic columns, the curve of which complements the semi-circular apse at the east end. Inside there is a flat ceiling with galleries on Ionic pillars; the decorative detail is inspired by Henry William's travels in Greece.

For long known as the Camden Chapel, All Saints took its present name in 1920. Since 1948 it has been on loan to the Greek Orthodox Church for the benefit of the Greek Cypriot Community.

RIGHT All Saints, Camden Town

BELOW All Hallows, Savernake Road

CHRIST THE KING
Gordon Square, WC1
(John Raphael Brandon, 1850-54)

The Church of Christ the King was built in the 1850s as the Catholic Apostolic Church of the Irvingites, a sect – founded some thirty years before by a Presbyterian Scot, Edward Irving – which had practised nonconformist ritualism and was governed by a college of 'apostles' with the gift of tongues. Irving himself, a friend of Thomas Carlyle, had preached the imminent end of the world.

The design was by John Raphael Brandon, an ardent exponent of the Gothic Revival style, which is displayed here on an imposing scale. The cruciform interior is huge: 212 feet long by 77 feet wide, with a nave 90 feet high. It is constructed in Bath stone, with a groined chancel and presbytery beneath a hammerbeam roof. Distinctive features are the 'angels throne' (similar to a bishop's throne) and the seven lamps that still hang before the altar in accordance with Catholic Apostolic practice. Although the sect has now dwindled away, Christ the King remains unaltered as a condition of the lease granted in 1963 to the University of London, whose church it is today.

ABOVE Christ the King, Gordon Square

LEFT All Saints, Camden Town

RIGHT Holy Trinity, Kingsway

HOLY TRINITY
Kingsway (between Parker Street and
Portugal Street), WC2
(John Belcher and J. J. Joass, 1909-11)

A church known as Holy Trinity, Little Queen Street, used to stand near this site. It had been built by Francis Bedford in 1829–31, but in 1909 it was undermined by the building of the Piccadilly Line underground and subsequently demolished. The present place of worship, one of the very few examples of an Edwardian Baroque church, was erected between 1909–11 to the designs of John Belcher and J. J. Joass who modelled it on Pietro da Cortona's S. Maria della Pace in Rome.

The building has a concave façade with a semi-circular projecting portico topped by a shallow dome. It was never entirely finished as money ran out, and behind the porch, in place of the intended tower, there rises a funny little bellcote. There was

also no money for the stone facing to the interior, and this is therefore very plain with white-washed walls below and exposed brick above. Holy Trinity has been declared redundant and is now closed.

◆

LINCOLN'S INN CHAPEL
Chancery Lane, WC2
(John Clarke, 1620-23)

The present Chapel was built between 1620–23 to replace an earlier one which had served the legal fraternity of Lincoln's Inn since medieval times. It is in the Perpendicular style and although often attributed to Inigo Jones was, in fact, designed by the mason, John Clarke. There are Victorian additions at the west end. The foundation stone was laid by John Donne who, as Dean of St Paul's, preached the consecration sermon on Ascension Day 1623.

The Gothic undercroft which supports the structure is built with low open arches. It was intended for use as a sort of sheltered common-room and meeting-place and it was here, in 1659, that eighty Members of Parliament met secretly to discuss

plans for a restored monarchy. It was here too, soon after their hopes had been realised, that Samuel Pepys strolled about having first admired 'the new garden which they are making and will be very pretty'.

Internment in the Chapel had always been confined to males, but in 1839 Lord Brougham petitioned successfully to have his daughter, Tullia, buried here so that he might later lie beside her. However, his death took place at his château at Cannes and he was buried in the cemetery there.

The interior is much restored but is notable for its beautiful dark box pews, most with their original pew ends complete with poppyheads. A large number of heraldic emblems are displayed in stained glass in several windows. The pulpit and communion table are early eighteenth-century.

◆

ST DOMINIC'S PRIORY
Southampton Road, NW5
(Charles Buckler, 1874-83)

A Dominican Priory was opened here in 1867, on the edge of the rapidly developing area of Kentish

ABOVE and LEFT Lincoln's Inn Chapel

RIGHT St George's, Bloomsbury

Town. Church services were originally held in the large Priory hall, but the Roman Catholic population in the surrounding areas became so large that it was decided to build a church. Though the foundation stone of The Priory Church of Our Lady of the Rosary and St Dominic's was laid in 1863, real work on the building began only in 1874, and the church was not finally opened until 1883. The architect was Charles Buckler who built a huge, towerless church 200 feet long, with sixteen side chapels and a roof nearly eighty feet high. One of the largest Roman Catholic churches in London, it was called in 1904 'the pride of all North London Roman Catholics'. Inside is a column from the pre-Reformation Dominican Church which stood on the site of the present-day Blackfriars Station. There is a fine Willis organ.

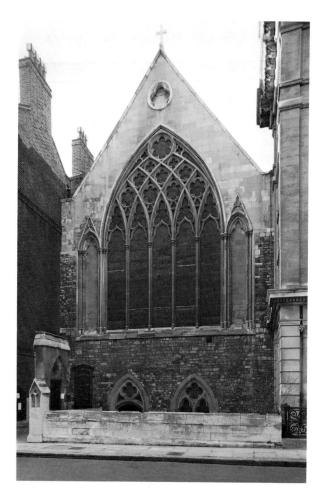

restored in a manner appropriate to its age. It is one of the very few medieval churches which belong to the Roman Catholics.

◆

ST GEORGE'S, BLOOMSBURY
Bloomsbury Way, WC1
(Nicholas Hawksmoor, 1720-30)

St George's is dedicated to the patron saint of England who was martyred in 303 AD. But the figure on the top of the steeple is George I, masquerading in Roman dress, whose statue inspired the lines:

> *When Henry the Eighth left the Pope in the lurch*
> *The Protestants made him the Head of the Church;*
> *But George's good subjects, the Bloomsbury people,*
> *Instead of the Church, made him head of the*
> *Steeple.*

The steeple in question was part of Nicholas Hawksmoor's new church, sanctioned by the Fifty New Churches Act of 1711 to relieve the par-

ST ETHELDREDA'S
Ely Place, EC1

The dedication refers to a seventh-century Abbess of Ely, and it was as a chapel to the London house of the Bishops of Ely that the present late thirteenth-century church was built. During the reign of Elizabeth I, the then Bishop was dispossessed of his London property by one of the Queen's courtiers and favourites, Sir Christopher Hatton. Episcopalian wrath was met by strong words from Her Majesty: 'I would have you know that I, who made you what you are, can unmake you and if you do not forthwith fulfil your engagement, by God! I will immediately unfrock you.' The Bishop climbed down; but some time later the house and chapel were returned to the see of Ely with which they remained until 1722, when the house was demolished and the chapel became a proprietary chapel.

Thereafter it passed through several hands before it was bought in 1874 by the Rosminian Fathers. Although much of the original fabric has disappeared, St Etheldreda's has been very well

ishioners of the northern part of St Giles-in-the-Fields from having to cross a notorious district known as 'the Rookery' (depicted by Hogath in 'Gin Lane') to attend their parish church.

The church was completed in 1730 on a site, the length of which runs north to south. The magnificent exterior is faced with stone throughout, its principal façade displaying a grand portico, with vast Corinthian columns and huge pediment. The theme of columns and pediment is echoed in the tower but changes abruptly at the steeple stage, where it gives way to a stepped pyramid, inspired by Pliny's description of the Tomb of Mausolus at Halicarnassus. Statues of lions and unicorns once clambered round the angles at the base, but these were removed in 1871 by G. E. Street. The north façade has an enormous pediment over five bays, thickly columned with arched windows at the second stage.

Inside is a square centre, defined by Corinthian pillars and large depressed arches, which carry the

ABOVE and LEFT St George's, Bloomsbury

FAR LEFT St Etheldreda's

clerestory. Entrance is from the south into the back of the church which, because of its north–south axis, faces the altar. Hawksmoor had provided alternative designs for the altar site, and originally it stood in the east apse; but it was moved in 1781 to suit the convenience of the parishioners. The inlaid altarpiece came from the demolished Bedford House and was installed in about 1801.

Hawksmoor's work is much more admired today than in the past. In the eighteenth century, Horace Walpole dismissed St George's as 'a masterpiece of absurdity', and a hundred years later a London Guide (1876) commented that it enjoyed 'the privilege of being the most pretentious and ugliest edifice in the metropolis.'

ST GILES-IN-THE-FIELDS
St Giles High Street, WC2
(Henry Flitcroft, 1731-3)

The earliest place of worship here was probably a chapel attached to a hospital for lepers which was founded in 1101 by Matilda, wife of Henry I. By the thirteenth century, the chapel was also serving a local parish, although its status was not confirmed until 1547. A new brick church replaced the early building in the 1620s, but was in a ruinous state within a hundred years, undermined by an excessive number of burials – 3,216 of them in the year of the Great Plague alone.

The Fifty New Churches Commissioners agreed to pay for a new church on condition that the parishioners provided the stipend for the incumbent of St George's, Bloomsbury which was about to be built in the north of the parish. The judges of a competition held to select the architect awarded the commission to Henry Flitcroft who shared with his patron, Lord Burlington, an enthusiastic taste for the Palladian style. This is not, however, apparent in St Giles's which bears a strong resemblance to St Martin-in-the-Fields without the portico. The exterior is stone-faced with two tiers of windows, round-headed above, small rectangular below. The first storey is rusticated, and the copper roof is green. A tall steeple rises straight up from the façade, featuring a charming clock stage above the bell story. An 1804 archway at the front contains a relief, carved in 1687, showing the Resurrection of the Dead.

The interior also is similar to Gibbs's church with a wide tunnel vault, richly gilded groined aisle vaults springing from elegant corbels, and no clerestory. The decoration was renewed during a restoration by Norman Haines and Gordon Jackson in 1952–3. At the same time the circular font of 1810 was restored to St Giles's after a long absence in West Street Chapel. In it, in 1818, William and Clara Shelley, the infant children of the poet, and Allegra, daughter of Lord Byron and Claire Claremont, were christened. The organ, although much restored, is by Father Smith, 1671, in a case probably of 1734. The organ gallery bears the Royal Arms of George III. There is a sumptuous pulpit dating from 1676 which, although no longer a three-decker, is still a beautiful furnishing in inlaid mahogany. At the east end of the north aisle is another pulpit, very plain in comparison, which was also in the West Street Chapel where it was used by Wesley.

LEFT St Giles-in-the-Fields

BELOW St John's, Downshire Hill

The garden to the south of the church contains many tombstones with illegible inscriptions, but the 1678 memorial to George Chapman, erected by Inigo Jones to the translator of Homer, is no longer amongst them. Badly weathered, it has now been placed in the church. Andrew Marvell, who died in 1678, is also commemorated here.

◆

ST JOHN'S, DOWNSHIRE HILL
Downshire Hill, Hampstead, NW3
(1818)

This charming little proprietary chapel stands in a garden behind ornamental railings, on a small triangle of land formed by Keats Grove and Downshire Hill. It was built in 1818, probably to the designs of William Woods, a speculative builder who, with two partners, had bought the site in the preceding year. It was intended to serve the new middle-class development of pretty stuccoed houses in the vicinity. The first service was held in October 1823, and the first incumbent was the Rev. William Harness, a life-long friend of Lord Byron whom he had met at Harrow. The poet refrained from dedicating *Childe Harold* to him for fear of blemishing the reputation of a man whose goodness he greatly admired. In 1832 the chapel was peremptorily closed by Dr Samuel White, Vicar of Hampstead, who took exception to the Evangelical clergyman who had by then bought it. Ignoring the local outcry, Dr White, described by John Keats as 'the parson of Hampstead quarrelling with all the world', refused to reopen St John's until 1835 when a more compliant incumbent was found for it. In 1916 the freehold of the chapel was bought by Leslie Wright, who leased it to the congregation for a nominal rent. At his death he requested that it should not be sold so long as there was a congregation to support a minister and maintain the building. It remains today the only proprietary chapel in the diocese of London which is self-supporting. Although licensed for baptisms in 1890, it cannot be used for the celebration of marriage except by archbishop's licence.

Its exterior is faced with stucco with a wooden bell-turret, its white classical façade embellished with a clock and a plaque bearing the church's name. The simple interior is also painted white

and is very light, with a barrel-vaulted ceiling flattened over the galleries which rest on cast-iron columns. In keeping with the Evangelical tradition, there is no recessed chancel; in a recent renovation, Biblical texts around the frieze of the gallery and reredos, obscured by paint in 1923, were revealed and restored. A notable feature is the box pews which have umbrella stands on their doors.

◆

ST JOHN'S, HAMPSTEAD
Church Row, Hampstead, NW3
(John Sanderson, 1745-7)

The medieval church of St John's, first mentioned in 1312 although probably founded earlier, had been out of repair for many years when, in 1744, the vestry decided to build a new one, the expense to be borne by the parish. Henry Flitcroft, a parishioner, had offered his services free; but as he was unwilling to take part in a competition, these were rejected, and John Sanderson, another parishioner and fellow-architect, was appointed to design the new building. It was a questionable choice since, within five years of the church's completion, much of the woodwork had to be renewed because of damp; and in 1759 part of the steeple needed to be rebuilt because the mason had used Purbeck instead of Portland stone. The battlements were built at that time, the copper spire being added in 1784. In 1874 a proposal to pull down the east tower to make way for the almost mandatory Victorian chancel was met with stubborn and influential opposition. A petition, organised by George Gilbert Scott the Younger, declared that the church and the houses in Church Row made such a harmonious whole that 'the proposal to destroy or transform its principal ornament will be condemned by every man of taste'. To his own signature were added those of Norman Shaw, William Butterfield, J. P. Seddon, Alfred Waterhouse, William Morris, William Holman Hunt, Anthony Trollope and Dante Gabriel Rossetti. The matter was dropped and when, three years later, St John's was enlarged by F. P. Cockerell the tower was left undisturbed. In a reversal of orientation the chancel was placed at the west end, and at the same time the nave was

RIGHT St John's, Hampstead

redecorated by Alfred Bell whose Renaissance style is well adapted to the rounded windows and vaulting of the interior. The wooden chancel furnishings are by T. G. Jackson.

The plain yellow brick church stands amid churchyard yews, the reprieved tower still forming the view for the handsome houses it overlooks. The wrought-iron gates, placed at the entry to the graveyard in 1747, were bought from the sale of Canons Park, Stanmore, the house of the Duke of Chandos, and within them lie buried the bodies of John Constable, Norman Shaw, George du Maurier, Sir Herbert Beerbohm Tree and Hugh Gaitskell.

◆

St Katharine's, Regent's Park

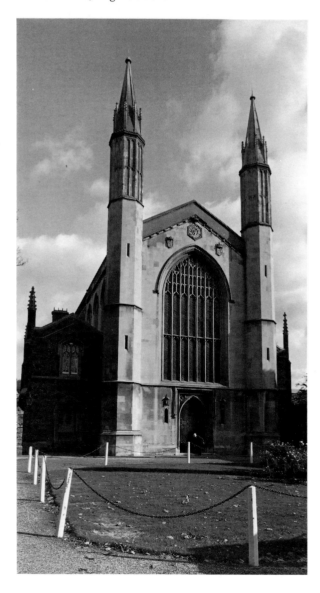

ST KATHARINE'S, REGENT'S PARK
Outer Circle, Regent's Park, NW1
(Ambrose Poynter, 1829)

The chapel that formed part of the religious hospice, founded in 1148 by Queen Matilda and later known as the Hospital of St Katharine, was removed from its ancient site by the Tower in 1825 to make way for the development of St Katharine's Dock. The Hospital was re-established in the following year among the new Nash terraces of Regent's Park, and Ambrose Poynter was invited to design the new chapel for them. The style of the present church is Perpendicular, and the façade, in stock brick, displays two tall narrow turrets set on either side of the nave.

The patronage of the chapel had always rested with the Queen of England (whether Sovereign or Consort), and it was Queen Alexandra, the Danish wife of King Edward VII, who granted it to the Danish community in London. It remains today their principal church.

Inside, it is whitewashed, furnished with Scandinavian pale wood fittings and contains seventeenth-century figures of Moses and John the Baptist, carved out of wood by Caius Cibber, which came from the old Danish Church in Wellclose Square, E1. A copy of the Rune stone, set up at Jelling in about 980 AD by Harold Bluetooth, first Christian King of Denmark, stands outside the church.

◆

ST MARTIN'S, VICAR'S ROAD,
Gospel Oak, NW5 (E. B. Lamb, 1865-6)

Built and largely paid for by a local resident, J. D. Allcroft, a glove manufacturer, St Martin's, which was designed by E. B. Lamb and consecrated in 1866, has an originality and eccentricity all its own. Indeed, Nikolaus Pevsner calles it 'the craziest of London's Victorian churches', having 'a whole which is both striking and harrowing'. The tower is immensely tall, although the four turrets which once decorated it had to be removed after bomb damage in the Second World War. The roof is gabled; the windows are tall and Tudor. Inside, the amazing hammerbeam roof is borne on shafts which end, not on the ground, but on Cistercian-like brackets; these brackets are attached to each side of the huge square piers which stand between nave and aisles.

St Mary Magdalene, Munster Square

ST MARY'S
Holly Place, Hampstead, NW3
(1815-16)

In 1792 the Abbé Morel, together with other French priests who refused to take the oath to the post-Revolution French Constitution, took refuge in England. In 1796, learning that many French refugee families were living in Hampstead, he decided to set up a church for them. For some time he held services in Oriel House in Church Row, but by 1815 enough money had been raised to build a church. The attractive small chapel, set in a row of terraced cottages, was blessed and opened in August 1816. The gallery was enlarged in 1822 and in 1850 an open bellcote was added and a statue of the Virgin in Caen stone placed above the doorway. The Abbé Morel died in 1852 and was buried beneath the porch. General de Gaulle attended Mass here in the Second World War while he was living in nearby Frognal.

ST MARY MAGDALENE, MUNSTER SQUARE
Munster Square, NW1
(Richard Cromwell Carpenter, 1849-52)

St Mary Magdalene stands in a corner of what used to be known as York Square, an area which, in the mid-nineteenth century, had acquired a rather disreputable character. It was founded by the Rev. Edward Stuart, a well-to-do young curate of Christ Church, Albany Street, whose aim was to build a church, 'as nearly perfection as the handicraft of man, the skill of architects, and the experience of ecclesiastical art could make it'. The architect was R. C. Carpenter whose design in the Decorated Gothic style so much admired by Ruskin, was described by the *Ecclesiologist* in 1852 as 'the most artistically correct new church yet consecrated in London'. The ragstone exterior is not spectacular and lacks the fine tower and spire originally planned for it. The interior, however, is beautifully proportioned, spacious and tall, with graceful arches, fine window tracery and white plastered walls. Later additions and embellishments have been made in the same devotional spirit; and Norman Shaw, a worshipper here for forty-two years, described it as, 'the beau ideal of a town church. In general aspect it is very restful, and is entirely free of all affectation in design'. Essentially unchanged, St Mary's remains unspoiled today.

◆

ST PANCRAS NEW CHURCH
Upper Woburn Place, WC1
(William Inwood and Henry
William Inwood, 1819-22)

The old village church of St Pancras could hold only about 150 people and so, in 1816, a new church was authorised by Act of Parliament to serve the increasing population in the by then urban area. It was built between 1819–22 by the Inwoods, father and son, in a neo-Grecian style inspired by Henry William's study of Hellenic architecture during his travels in Greece. The Church of St Pancras was the first Greek Revival church to be built in London, and was also the most expensive since St Paul's Cathedral. Con-

structed in brick and stone-faced throughout, the exterior resembles the Acropolis temple known as the Erechtheum on which it is largely based. The tower, in diminishing octagons capped with finial and cross, is an adaptation of the Tower of the Winds at Athens. The huge Ionic portico fronting the oblong building is answered by a rounded apse at the east end beyond which project, on either side, duplicate porticos, each housing a vestry and each, in place of columns, having a row of draped female figures made in terracotta with cast-iron stanchions inside. Internally, the church is like a great hall, flat-ceilinged with low straight galleries. Six Ionic columns support the organ gallery, and six more – in most impressive fashion – ring the apse. The detail throughout is scrupulously accurate, the furnishings beautifully made and, since the removal in a 1950s restoration of some oppressive Victorian decoration, the church is much lighter than formerly. The stained glass by Clayton and Bell was retained, the glass in the windows behind the altar being particularly good.

St Pancras Church is one of the great representative works of the Greek Revival. According to Sir John Summerson writing in 1952, 'St Pancras, both in its loyalties and its originalities, its scholarship and its natural dignity, is *the* parish church of Regency London'.

◆

ST PANCRAS OLD CHURCH
Pancras Road, NW1

Maximilian Misson, an early eighteenth-century travel writer, considered 'St Pancrace, under Highgate near London' to be a Christian foundation more ancient even than the early fourth-century St John Lateran in Rome. Certainly the area has been recognised as a parish since the ninth century, although the first reliable reference to a place of worship here is not until the second half of the twelfth century.

For hundreds of years, St Pancras's was just a little country village church which seems to have been almost abandoned at times in its history. Writing in 1593, John Norden, the map publisher,

LEFT St Pancras New Church

RIGHT St Pancras Old Church

describes it standing '... all alone as utterly forsaken, old and weatherbeaten, which for the antiquity thereof, it is thought not to yield to Paule's in London; about this church have been many buildings now decayed, leaving poor Pancras without company or comfort.' He adds a cautionary note, 'Yet it is visited by thieves, who assemble there not to pray, but to wait for prey ... Walk not there too late.'

During the seventeenth century, the parish was not held in much esteem. 'Thou Pancridge Parson' was a term of derision in 1612, and Inigo Jones was roundly abused as 'Pancridge Earl and Marquis of Tower Ditch' by Ben Jonson with whom he had quarrelled. The church also acquired a reputation for laxity in the matter of illegal marriages, the churchyard was said to be the scene of duelling, and towards the end of the century the vicar was imprisoned for debt.

The structure of the present church dates mainly from the fourteenth century, but the exterior was given such a thorough going-over by Gough and Roumieu in 1847–8 that its appearance today is more Victorian than medieval. Subsequent restorations, the last during the late 1970s, have managed to leave intact the village atmosphere of the interior, which is enhanced by a muster of ancient monuments and a sixth-century altar-stone, uncovered during the nineteenth-century alterations.

The churchyard, now merged with the former burial ground of St Giles-in-the-Fields, is a public garden in which the graves of famous and infamous jostle promiscuously together. It seems to have been a favoured resting place for murderers, blackmailers, pimps and thieves. One epitaph, preserved by F. T. Cansick in *Epitaphs of Middlesex* (1869) and now no longer legible, used to read: 'The mortal remains of John Brindle; after an evil life of 64 years, died June 18th 1822 and lies at rest beneath this stone.' In contrast is the splendid tomb erected by Sir John Soane to his wife who died in 1815, which records a veritable catalogue of her virtues. Sir John was buried here beside her in 1837. Also buried here was Johann Christian Bach (died 1782); the sculptor, John Flaxman (died 1826); William Godwin (died 1836) and his two wives. His first wife, Mary Wollstonecraft, died in 1797 after childbirth, and her daughter, Mary Godwin, met her future husband, P. B. Shelley, while visiting her mother's grave. The remains of Mary Wollstonecraft were transferred to Bournemouth in 1851. A number of aristocratic French refugees were also interred here. Charles

Dickens's *A Tale of Two Cities* contains an episode in which the corpse of an Old Bailey spy is brought by hearse to 'the old church of Saint Pancras, far off in the fields', only to be removed later by body snatchers.

After the building in 1822 of St Pancras New Church, the old church was for a time a chapel of ease; but in 1863 it was reinstated as a parish church and since 1956 the parish has been combined with that of St Matthew, Oakley Square.

◆

ST STEPHEN'S, ROSSLYN HILL
The Green, Rosslyn Hill, NW3
(S. S. Teulon, 1869-76)

Built by S.S. Teulon between 1869–76, St Stephen's was highly praised in its day by Charles Eastlake in his *History of the Gothic Revival* (1872), although it has come in for some stringent criticism since. It is a huge building in brick of weathered purple, dressed with granite and stone. The impression is one of weight and vigour; the style, rooted in Gothic, is triumphantly High Victorian. But how long it survives depends on

whether a use for it can be found. Since 1977, St Stephen's has been redundant, and at the present time (1987) is boarded up.

◆

WHITEFIELD'S TABERNACLE
Tottenham Court Road, W1 (1756)

Whitefield's Tabernacle was named after the famous Methodist preacher, George Whitefield, for whom it was built in 1756. So popular were his sermons that in 1760 the front of the building was extended to accommodate the enormous crowds that flocked to hear him. Although it was ridiculed as 'Whitefield's soul trap', the Tabernacle attracted many admirers from the *haut monde*, among them Horace Walpole, Lord Bolingbroke and David Hume.

It has been rebuilt several times since its heyday, the last time after the Second World War. It is now the American Church in London.

LEFT St Stephen's, Rosslyn Hill

BELOW Whitefield's Tabernacle

Two other interesting churches in Camden are William Butterfield's St Albans, Holborn, EC1 (1859–62) and St Michael's, Camden Road, NW1 by G. F. Bodley and T. Garner in English Decorated Gothic (1880–94).

St Albans, Holborn

HACKNEY

◆

ST JOHN AT HACKNEY
Mare Street, E8 (James Spiller, 1797)

The parish church at Hackney was formerly known as St Augustine's, and its present name has only with certainty been attached to it since 1660. The old church, founded in the late thirteenth century, was rebuilt several times, and by the 1790s was too small to support a parish enlarged by a growing number of private schools in the area. The new Church, by James Spiller, was built on a fresh site in the churchyard, to the north-east of the sixteenth-century ragstone tower which was left standing when the former church was demolished. Spiller's church is very large, sombre and magnificent in brown brick with a stone steeple, which was added some years later, together with the east

St John at Hackney

window and semi-circular porches. The plan is a Greek cross, almost square, with the merest projections. The main façade shows a large semi-circular porch, huge brick pediment and a white tower in diminishing square stages, crowned by what Sir Nikolaus Pevsner called 'a motif that defeats description'.

There has been considerable rearrangement of the interior since its restoration after a fire which gutted the building in 1955. The large galleries still remain, spreading back to the north, south and west sides in the form of a horseshoe, and contained by a railing. But the present high altar now stands in a small circular sanctuary, and there is a new east window by Christopher Webb (1958). The size of this huge church is rather an embarrassment today, although an attempt has been made to fill it with a war memorial chapel under one part of the south gallery and a new clergy vestry under another. A few fine monuments, relics from the old church, are housed in the north vestibule.

◆

ST LEONARD'S, SHOREDITCH
Shoreditch High Street and Hackney Road, E1 (George Dance the Elder, 1736-40)

St Leonard's belonged in the twelfth century to the Priory of the Holy Trinity, Aldgate. It may well have stood on the site of an even earlier church. The living passed through various hands to the Archdeacon of London with whom it still rests. The church's early history was linked with two local theatres, the Curtain and the Theatre, and references to births, deaths and marriages of actors abound – so much so that in Elizabethan times St Leonard's became known as the Actors' Church. Richard Burbage was buried here.

By the early eighteenth century, the medieval building had become hazardous, with bits of the fabric falling off during services. In 1716 one of the corners of the tower collapsed with a fearful noise, causing panic amongst the congregation. It was patched up, but as the church was also considered insanitary (being below pavement level) it was eventually decided to rebuild it. The architect was George Dance the Elder, and his ambitious design was to form a landmark in the neighbourhood. His church stands at a crossroads,

and its tall, slender steeple (192 feet high) still dominates the landscape. It is in stone with an elongated cupola, small lantern and square obelisk, reminiscent in appearance of the steeple of St Mary-le-Bow. Its position, astride a huge Tuscan portico, derives, however, from Gibbs's St Martin-in-the-Fields. The body of the church is brick with stone dressings. Although the removal of the north and south galleries in 1857 distorted the proportions of the interior, it has not significantly altered the design of lofty nave, low clerestory and Tuscan arcades. An organ gallery at the west end contains a clock with an exceptionally beautiful surround. There is an outstanding memorial to Elizabeth Benson who died in 1710 aged 89; it is a ghoulish composition of skeletons pulling at the uprooted Tree of Life over which is hooked a shroud.

St Leonard's, in 1817, was the first church in London to be lit by gas; it is now illuminated by pendant neon tubes. Furnishings include a handsome carved pulpit, hexagonal in shape with tester and staircase; a very fine carved font cover with

ABOVE Organ gallery clock, St Leonard's, Shoreditch

RIGHT St Leonard's, Shoreditch

an unusual pulley attachment and a circular marble font on a pedestal. Only the modern-looking architrave spanning the nave (probably added in a restoration of 1933) seems, with its complement of plaster figures, to be out of keeping with the rest of the attractive interior.

This is the church whose bells, according to nursery lore, rang out, 'When I grow rich, say the bells of Shoreditch'. Elizabeth and Wayland Young in their book *Old London Churches* extracted the following lines from verses written by a team of ringers who visited the old church shortly before its demolition:

The peal of bells are not extra ornary
For some are very ornary
They'd be much better if they had
A good second and third, for those are bad.

In those days there were twelve bells, but in 1963

a thirteenth was donated by the Haberdashers' Company.

St Leonard's has often been restored, the last time in 1963 when it was completely re-decorated.

◆

ST MARK'S, DALSTON
Sandringham Road, E8
(Chester Cheston, 1886;
Tower, E. L. Blackburne, 1877)

St Mark's has been described as a good example of a mid-Victorian Evangelical church, that is, built in the Early English style but not too fastidious as to detail. Little is known about its architect, Chester Cheston, but perhaps it is significant that when funds permitted, another architect, E. L. Blackburne, was invited to design the tower. This is a splendid affair with turret, pinnacles, contrasting brick and stone, and a clock stage which shows a barometer on one of its faces.

The interior is very wide, the arcades supported on clusters of thin iron columns with ingenious capitals. The chancel is short, richly decorated and has a mosaic reredos. A singular and picturesque feature of the church is the stained glass panels filled with blue sky and golden angels, which are set into the spandrels of the nave roof above the transept. The furnishings are very good, and there is an abundance of notched brick and polychromatic decoration throughout. A charming touch is the lighting, provided from fittings adapted from the original gasoliers.

◆

ST MARY'S, STOKE NEWINGTON
Stoke Newington Church Street, N16
(Old Church, 1563; New Church,
George Gilbert Scott, 1854-58)

Standing in close proximity and striking contrast to each other are the two churches of St Mary, Stoke Newington. The foundation of the Old Church is ancient, going back at least 1,000 years, although little is known about the early building (or buildings). However, in 1563, 'the Parish Church of Stokenwenton, being ruinous', was rebuilt by William Peter, Lord of the Manor, and

LEFT St Mark's, Dalston

BELOW St Mary's Old Church, Stoke Newington

the present church dates from that time, although generally enlarged in the late 1820s by Sir Charles Barry. Under his direction a north aisle, clerestory and shingled spire were added. Often repaired and much restored – the last time after bomb damage received in the Second World War – St Mary's, standing in its leafy churchyard, has still the appearance of a country village church: Tudor red brick outside, box pews within.

Although St Mary's Old Church is still in active use, it has not been parochial for more than a century, its parish status having been transferred to St Mary's New Church in 1858. From Clissold Park there is a view of both churches, the large Victorian one towering above and behind its little predecessor.

The New Church was built to accommodate the huge crowds which were drawn from all over London in the 1850s to hear the preaching of the rector, the Rev. Thomas Jackson. Initial proposals involving the demolition of the Old Church had been opposed, and the new building, designed by George Gilbert Scott and financed by voluntary subscription, was constructed in the garden of the old Rectory on the other side of Church Street. It is in the thirteenth-century Gothic style, conceived in the grand manner with wide nave, lofty arcades, plentiful use of marble and ostentatious

furnishings. The enormously tall spire was not added for another thirty years, and the long delay gave rise to the rhyme:

Stoke Newington is a funny place
With lots of funny people
Thomas Jackson built a church
But could not build a steeple.

The steeple was, in fact, completed by the architect's son, John Oldrid Scott, in 1890.

St Mary New Church was badly damaged during the Second World War, and was afterwards restored by yet another member of the Scott family, Charles Marriott Oldrich Scott. It was reconsecrated in 1957.

◆

ST MATTHIAS'S
Wordsworth Road, N16
(William Butterfield, 1851-3)

Although the *Ecclesiologist* gave almost unqualified approval to William Butterfield's remarkable design for the church of St Matthias, exhibited in 1850, there were some harsh strictures on it from other quarters: the saddleback tower over the chancel was awkward, the aisles were too low, and the west front with its central buttress bisecting the west window was a decadent imitation of a medieval precedent (Dorchester Abbey, Oxfordshire). Butterfield removed some offending pinnacles from the plan and the church was built between 1851–3. He gave his services free of charge, his workmen refused overtime pay and St Matthias was completed for only £7,000. All the seats were free, which perhaps accounted for the numbers who attended its consecration in June 1853. An issue of the *Guardian* commented: 'Notwithstanding the unfortunate nature of the weather, the sittings were completely filled, and indeed many were forced to be content with standing-room.'

The church is impressive both outside and in. The gable of the towering west front is repeated in the sharply pitched roof of the steeple in an arresting composition which is completed by the low aisles on either side. The interior, of great height and severe beauty, is equally imposing. After the Second World War there were plans to demolish the damaged churches of both St Matthias and its neighbour, St Faith, and replace them with one new church. Great was the outcry, and eventually St Faith's was pulled down and St Matthias's restored. It has been correctly rebuilt but without its former decoration. Stripped of the original polychrome, the noble outlines of the structure are fully revealed.

◆

Also in Hackney is St Mary of Eton, Hackney Wick, built in the 1890s to the designs of C. F. Bodley with funds provided by Eton College; the gate-tower is by Cecil Hare (1911–12).

◆

BELOW and LEFT St Mary's New Church, Stoke Newington

ISLINGTON

St James's, Clerkenwell

ST CLEMENT'S, BARNSBURY
St Clement's Street, N7
(George Gilbert Scott, 1863-5)

Sir Nikolaus Pevsner described St Clement's as 'far less conventional and well-bred than most of Scott's work'. It was built at the expense of a Mr Cubitt, and was designed to offer the inhabitants of Islington an alternative to the form of evangelical worship prevailing in their local church. It is in stock brick with stone dressings and three red brick porches. The west front is tall and steep with buttresses and a bell-turret, below which is a niche containing the seated figure of St Clement. At the east end are three lancet windows. In the 1970s, St Clement's was made redundant, and in 1986 it was converted into 23 flats. The exterior has been cleaned and refurbished, and is left unaltered except for small window-lights let into the roof.

ST JAMES'S, CLERKENWELL
Clerkenwell Green, EC1
(James Carr, 1788-92)

St James's was once a part of a Benedictine nunnery which was founded in about 1100 and to which the dedication to St James was added in about 1500. The nunnery was dissolved in 1539 and all the buildings, apart from the church, were pulled down. The church itself was subsequently rebuilt but before the end of the eighteenth century had become ruinous and was also then demolished. It was rebuilt in 1788–92 by James Carr who was responsible for the odd stone facing on the west front and the graceful interior. The children's galleries, made of iron, were inserted in 1822 and the spire was rebuilt in 1849 by W. P. Griffith. The church was sympathetically restored by Sir Arthur Blomfield in 1882. Bishop Burnet, the historian, was buried here in 1715.

◆

ST JOHN'S, CLERKENWELL
St John's Square, EC1

A priory church was built here in about 1145 by the crusading order of the Knights Hospitaller of St John. It had a round nave with a small rectangular chancel and crypt below, and was consecrated by Heraclius, the Patriarch of Jerusalem, in 1185. The Priory was burned down and its Prior murdered during the Peasants' Revolt of 1381, and, having been rebuilt, it fell into decay again after the Dissolution of the Monasteries when most of the church was blown up to provide stone for Somerset House. The chancel survived, however, eventually to become the property of Lord Burleigh whose wife turned it into a private chapel which was opened for worship in 1623. In 1706 it became a Presbyterian meeting-house, and, in repetition of its early history, was burned and gutted during the Sacheverell Riots of 1710. Thereafter it was reclaimed by Simon and Charity Michel who sold it in 1723 to the Commissioners of the Fifty New Churches under whom it became, and remained for 200 years, parochial.

The decline in number of local residents caused it to be deprived of parish status in 1929, and it

RIGHT St Mary's, Islington

ABOVE St John's, Clerkenwell

LEFT Figure of Juan Ruyz de Vergara, St John's, Clerkenwell

now belongs to the Order of St John of Jerusalem, the organisation founded in the reign of Queen Victoria. Gutted in 1941, St John's was rebuilt by Lord Mottistone in the 1950s. The 1721 red brick exterior which survived the bombing is quite plain, and the outline of the original round nave is marked in cobbles on the pavement outside. The interior is brilliant with red seat coverings and banners of the Order. There are two outstanding monuments which have been preserved: one, a 1575 figure, in alabaster, of Juan Ruyz de Vergara of the Langue of Castile, came from Valladolid Cathedral; the other is an effigy of Sir William Weston, last Prior of the Order of the Knights Hospitaller who is said to have died of a broken heart at the Dissolution. John Wilkes was married here in 1747, and Queen Victoria's cousin the Duke of Cambridge married the actress Sarah Fairbrother in 1840.

The ancient crypt, which has survived so much, is still used for services and may be seen, together with the rest of the church, with permission from the Curator of the Library and Museum at St John's Gate.

ST MARY'S, ISLINGTON
Upper Street, Islington, N1
(Launcelot Dowbiggin, 1751-4;
rebuilt, Seely and Paget, 1954-6)

The foundation of St Mary's, Islington is extremely old: there is mention of a place of worship here in the twelfth century. The medieval church which succeeded it survived until 1751, when it was found dangerous and taken down. Petitions for another church had been ignored for more than thirty years, but in 1750 a new one was sanctioned by Act of Parliament and a local master-joiner, Launcelot Dowbiggin, was appointed architect.

All that survives of Dowbiggin's church since the bombing of 1940 is the tower, a lively composition showing a diversity of styles: square tower, octagonal balustrade, open circle of columns, conical dome and rusticated obelisk spire. Not only is the tower something of an architectural curiosity but its history, too, is unusual. In 1787 it was shrouded in wickerwork instead of scaffolding while a lightning conductor was erected. So extraordinary was its appearance that people came from all over London to see it, and were charged 6d. for a view from the top by the contractor who made over £50. At the time, St Mary's was already becoming a centre of Evangelism. In 1738, Charles Wesley had begun his career as a preacher by becoming unlicensed lecturer here; in 1739 George Whitefield preached a sermon in the churchyard, after a churchwarden had denied him the use of the church. After his appointment as Vicar in 1824, Dr Daniel Wilson, later Bishop of Calcutta, started the Islington Clerical Meetings, from which grew the Islington Conference held annually at Church House, Westminster; and the modern church, built by Seely and Paget after the Second World War, continues the Evangelical tradition. Externally, it follows the old proportions except for the addition of small terminal transepts at the east end; it is in red brick with tall, rectangular windows and, of course, retains the original tower. The new interior, original and invigorating, is completely open with a spacious sanctuary separated from the transepts by slender, black fluted pillars. Most of the furnishings are modern, although the original font of veined marble, stored away since a restoration to the church in 1902–4, now stands in the south aisle.

In the churchyard, which is now a public

garden, lie the bodies of Sir George Wharton and Sir James Steward, a godson of James I, who killed each other in a duel and were interred in the same grave in 1609 by order of the King. Also buried here is Launcelot Dowbiggin who died in 1759.

◆

ST MICHAEL'S, HIGHGATE
South Grove, N6
(Lewis Vulliamy, 1830-32)

In medieval times a hermit's chapel, dedicated to St Michael, stood on Highgate Hill and served the inhabitants of Highgate as a chapel of ease to their parish church of Old St Pancras. When, in 1565, Highgate Grammar School was founded on the site by Sir Robert Cholmely, the ancient chapel was rebuilt as the School Chapel but continued to be used by the local residents until 1826, when it was closed to the public by the Lord Chancellor, Lord Eldon. Shortly afterwards, the present parish church of St Michael was built on a site in South Grove, which places it on higher ground than any other church in London, the entrance being level with the cross on the top of St Paul's Cathedral; its tall stone spire is clearly visible from the hills south of London. The body of the church is in

ABOVE Wesley's Chapel, with statue of John Wesley in the foreground

RIGHT St Michael's, Highgate

stock brick, the style Perpendicular.

A few monuments remain from the old Chapel, and a memorial in the main aisle marks the re-interment in 1961 of the body of Samuel Taylor Coleridge, originally buried in the School Chapel in 1834. The stained glass of the east window is one of the last works of Evie Hone who died in 1955.

◆

WESLEY'S CHAPEL
City Road (between Epworth Street
and Oliver's Yard), EC1 (1777-8)

For nearly forty years, John Wesley fed the hungry, cared for the sick and preached the gospel of Methodism to his followers in a converted foundry on Windmill Hill, Finsbury. When the lease of the foundry ran out, the present chapel in stock brick was built opposite Bunhill Fields. The foundation stone was laid by Wesley in 1777, and the chapel opened in the following year. Despite alterations and repairs during the nine-

St Saviour's, Aberdeen Park

teenth century, the building, which had survived unscathed the Second World War, was so decayed by 1972 as to be unfit for public use. Nearly £1 million was raised for its restoration and it was reopened in 1978.

Now beautifully renovated, the large, broad interior comes as a surprise. A horseshoe gallery on marble pillars takes up three sides, displaying below it a white and gold frieze featuring a dove and olive branch motif. The large central space is dominated by the handsome mahogany pulpit – set well forward on a raised marble and mosaic floor – which was Wesley's own. It is supported by four fluted pillars with rounded arches between them on three sides, and a staircase on the fourth.

Beside the front courtyard stands Wesley's

house, which is filled with memorabilia. The founder himself lies in a grave behind the chapel.

◆

Also of interest in Islington: St Saviour's, Aberdeen Park, Highbury, N5, a small brick church by William White (1865–6), recently restored; and St Mary Magdalene, Holloway, N7 (1812–14).

◆

WEST LONDON

◆

EALING

◆

HOLY CROSS, GREENFORD
Oldfield Lane, Greenford, Middlesex

There are two churches of the Holy Cross standing at right angles to each other in Oldfield Lane near Western Avenue. The old church dates from the late fifteenth or early sixteenth century but has been considerably altered. The exterior, in ragstone with stone dressings, has a weatherboard tower. It contains a font dating from 1638 and some notable early sixteenth-century glass, depicting the arms of Henry VII and Katharine of Aragon, transferred from King's College, Cambridge in the nineteenth century. The church was reprieved from demolition in 1951, extensively restored and reopened in 1956, and is still in use in conjunction with the new church of Holy Cross.

The new church, designed by Sir Albert Richardson and built between 1939–41 to accommodate the increasing population of Greenford, stands a little to the west of its medieval companion. The external walls, constructed in Stamford brick, are low and the tiled roof steeply pitched. The orientation is north-south. The interior is constructed mainly of Oregon pine.

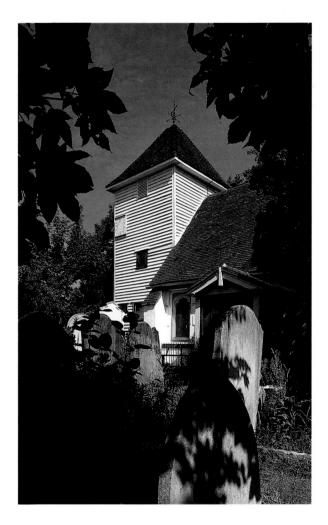

ABOVE St Mary the Virgin, Perivale

LEFT Holy Cross (old church), Greenford

ST MARY THE VIRGIN
Perivale Lane, Perivale, Middlesex

Now isolated from most of its former parish by the construction of Western Avenue, St Mary the Virgin is the last surviving building of the old village of Greenford Parva or Perivale. It was built in the twelfth century of flint and rag rubble with stone dressings but has been much altered over the years especially in the late fifteenth century and in a restoration of 1875. Like the nearby Holy Cross, Greenford, it has a pretty white-painted wooden tower which was added at the beginning of the sixteenth century. In the nineteenth century the graveyard was a fashionable resting place for the middle-class families of Ealing and there are also numerous wall monuments inside the church. This church has been closed for regular worship since 1972 and is now preserved by the Friends of St Mary's.

HAMMERSMITH & FULHAM

◆

ALL SAINTS, FULHAM
Putney Bridge Approach, Fulham, SW6
(Arthur Blomfield, 1880-81)

All Saints stands on ground that once was part of
the Manor of Fulham, owned by the Bishops of
London since the early eighth century. The site is
a splendid one, close by Putney Bridge looking
over the Thames. The first reliable mention of
a church here was in 1440 when the tower was
completed. The nineteenth century saw the demolition of the old place of worship, except for the
tower which had been refaced in 1845 and was
retained to form part of Arthur Blomfield's fine
new Gothic church of 1880–81 with which it har-
monizes admirably. The church, like the tower, is
battlemented, and both are built mainly of
Kentish ragstone with stone dressings.

The unexceptionable interior displays the usual
Perpendicular features, and is distinguished by

*RIGHT Memorial to Lady Margaret Legh, All Saints,
Fulham*

BELOW All Saints, Fulham

some extremely fine monuments. Ten Bishops of London lie in the large churchyard, and an eleventh, Bishop Henchman, is buried in the church itself.

◆

ST PAUL'S, HAMMERSMITH
Queen Caroline Street, W6
(Roumieu, Gough and Seddon, 1882-7)

There was no church in the hamlet of Hammersmith until 1629 when a chapel of ease to Fulham Church was built. It was consecrated by Bishop Laud in 1631 and was made parochial in 1834. The foundation stone of the present church was laid in July 1882, and the tower was completed and consecrated in July 1887. It is large and dignified, constructed in pink Mansfield stone with narrow lancet windows and a tall north-east tower sporting outsize pinnacles. The interior is well-proportioned and lofty with clustered columns of

RIGHT Bust of Charles I, St Paul's, Hammersmith

BELOW St Paul's, Hammersmith

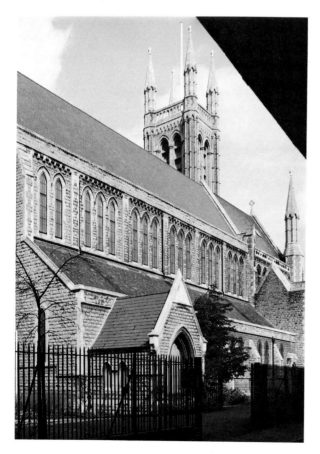

black marble; it contains two excellent monuments from the old church. One is a bust of Charles I which was erected to his memory by the Royalist, Sir Nicholas Crisp, whose own heart, after his death in 1665, reposed in an urn beneath the effigy of his beloved Monarch. For the next 150 years, it was customary to bring it out in a gruesome annual ceremony, 'to refresh it with a glass of wine'. The custom finally lapsed, and in 1898 the decayed heart was united with Crisp's body which was brought from its burial place in the City and interred here in the churchyard. North of the sanctuary is a fine memorial to James and Sarah Smith. There is a seventeenth-century pulpit which came from All Hallows the Great in 1900, and a font bowl, also seventeenth century, which is set on a ring of marble columns. Today, St Paul's is stranded in the midst of non-stop traffic and has to be reached by a subway.

◆

ST THOMAS'S, FULHAM
Rylston Road, Fulham SW6
(Augustus Welby Pugin, 1847-9)

St Thomas's was built by Elizabeth Bowden, a convert to Roman Catholicism, in memory of her husband, John. It was designed by Augustus Welby Pugin, himself a convert and an ardent exponent of the Gothic Revival. He is better known for his writings and engravings than for his actual buildings, so St Thomas's, one of his few London churches, should be of special interest. The exterior is picturesque in Kentish ragstone, constructed in the Decorated Perpendicular style. It has a fine pinnacled tower with an obelisk spire which faces into the churchyard. Inside, the decorative work suffered from a severely straitened budget; and, although the altars and pulpit are attractively adorned with figures and foliage, the general impression of the interior is disappointing.

◆

Also of interest in Hammersmith and Fulham: St Dionis's, Parson's Green, SW6, built in 1884–5 with the proceeds of the sale of the City Church of St Dionis Backchurch; and St Peter, Hammersmith, built in 1827-9 in Suffolk Brick by Edward Lapidge in a Grecian Style.

HOUNSLOW

◆

ST MICHAEL AND ALL ANGELS
Bedford Park, W4
(Norman Shaw, 1879-82)

Bedford Park, the artistic garden suburb pion-
eered by the property speculator, Jonathan Carr,
in the last quarter of the nineteenth century, combined avant-garde architecture with the cult of
the 'House Beautiful' in a movement away from
Victorian muscular Christianity and heavy seri-
ousmindedness. One of the principal architects
of this aesthetic vision was Norman Shaw, the
exterior of whose church displays a Queen Anne
prettiness particularly exemplified in its porch and
lantern. There is a suggestion of late Gothic about
the interior, which has a raised chancel and panelled dados to the walls and columns. It is very
much in keeping with its surroundings which are
little changed even today.

ABOVE St Nicholas's, Chiswick

LEFT St Michael and All Angels

FAR LEFT St Thomas's, Fulham

ST NICHOLAS'S, CHISWICK
Church Street, Chiswick, W4
(J. L. Pearson, 1882)

St Nicholas's stands beside the Thames close to
Chiswick Mall where, in ancient times, there was
a ford crossing. The present Gothic church was
built by J. L. Pearson in 1882, but the fifteenth-
century ragstone tower is a survival from an earlier
church. In the churchyard is buried Barbara Villi-
ers, created Duchess of Cleveland by Charles II
whose mistress she was. Her grave is not marked
by a memorial, but William Hogarth, who lived
nearby and is buried here too, is commemorated
by an urn on a massive pedestal.

◆

KENSINGTON & CHELSEA

ALL SAINTS, CHELSEA OLD CHURCH
Cheyne Walk, SW3

There seems to have been a Norman church on this site, but the dedication to All Saints is not recorded until 1290. The north chapel is of about 1325 and belonged to the Lord of the Manor of Chelsea who could see the altar through the squint still preserved in the east arch. The south chapel was rebuilt for his own private use in 1528 by Sir Thomas More to whom there is a monument in the sanctuary where his first wife's Gothic altar tomb is also to be found. Among other memorials in the church are the badly damaged tomb of the Duchess of Northumberland, mother-in-law of Lady Jane Grey, a sculpture to Chelsea's benefactress Lady Jane Cheyne, and a memorial plaque to Henry James.

The church was severely damaged by bombing in 1941 when five firewatchers were killed. The restoration was carried out under the direction of Walter Godfrey. Still preserved in the church are the seventeenth-century altar and barley sugar rails, the 1673 marble font and six chained books, the only chained books in any London church, the gift of Sir Hans Sloane whose monument by Joseph Wilton is in the churchyard. The bell hanging in the porch was given in 1679 in thanksgiving for safety from drowning by 'William Ashburnham esqvier Cofferer to his Majesties household'.

THE BROMPTON ORATORY
Brompton Road (next to Victoria and Albert Museum), SW3 (Herbert Gribble, 1880-84)

The oratory of St Philip Neri, founded in Rome in the sixteenth century, was introduced into England in 1848 by John Henry Newman and Frederick William Faber and established in London and Birmingham.

All Saints, Chelsea Old Church with statue of Sir Thomas More in the foreground

The design of the London Oratory is the result of a competition held in 1878 and won by Herbert Gribble, a hitherto unknown architect. The church he built replaced a temporary place of worship by J. J. Scoles. The sponsors had stipulated an Italian Renaissance design, and Gribble's scheme succeeds in conveying an atmosphere of High Baroque although the style is designated Italian Mannerist. Outside a large dome, pinnacles, pilasters and pediment combine to give the appearance of a cathedral. Inside, there is a nave and side chapels, much rich Italian decoration and a number of late seventeenth-century furnishings, including the Lady Altar, the Altar of St Wilfrid and twelve huge marble figures of the Apostles by G. Mazzuoli (circa 1680–85) which came from the Cathedral at Siena. The black and white altarpiece in the Chapel of the Seven Dolours is by Gribble himself; in the Chapel of the English Martyrs there is a fine triptych by Rex Whistler. The ancillary buildings consist of the Oratorian house at the back of the church, built by J. J. Scoles in 1853, and St Wilfrid's Hall (1910) by A. Stokes to its left. In front of this is a 1896 statue of Cardinal Newman, the work of Bodley and Garner. The funeral of Cardinal Manning was held at the Oratory in 1892.

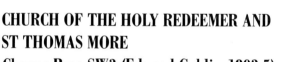

CHURCH OF THE HOLY REDEEMER AND ST THOMAS MORE
Cheyne Row, SW3 (Edward Goldie, 1893-5)

This is one of the few Victorian Roman Catholic churches to have been built in the Classical tradition. The architect, Edward Goldie, a devotee of the Gothic style, had been reluctant to follow it, but had been persuaded to do so by his client, Canon Cornelius Keen. Shortages of money and limitations of site had precluded a domed church in the Oratorian manner, and there were criticisms of its bleak 'concert hall' appearance when the Church of the Holy Redeemer was opened in 1895. The dedication to St Thomas More was added in 1935 after his canonisation, and an altar containing a bone from his vertebrae was put up in his honour.

HOLY TRINITY, LATIMER ROAD
Shalfleet Drive, W10
(Norman Shaw, 1887-9)

The Church of Holy Trinity, built as the Manor School Mission by Norman Shaw in a style veering towards 'Queen Anne', is a large brick building with one great gable and two huge windows, delicately traceried, to the east and west. Now redundant, it has been converted into a boys' club.

HOLY TRINITY
Sloane Street (between Sloane Terrace and Sloane Square), SW1
(John Dando Sedding, 1889-90)

The Church of the Holy Trinity, built between 1889–90, replaced an earlier Gothic church designed by James Savage in 1830 as a chapel of ease to his church of St Luke in Sydney Street. The present church, embodying the principles of

Church of the Holy Redeemer and St Thomas More

the Arts and Crafts Movement inspired by William Morris, is John Dando Sedding's last work. Apart from the front, the exterior walls are of the plainest brickwork. The principal façade, constructed in brick and stone, is embattled with four turrets, and given symmetry by the projection of the right-hand porch beyond the aisle. Inside there is a wide vaulted nave with a chancel of the same width and height and non-symmetrical aisles, the northern one being wider than the one to the south. It is built in a style which, while loosely Gothic, displays a blend of fourteenth- and fifteenth-century features with even a hint of Renaissance in a composition which is Sedding's very own. As a building it is remarkable; but in its adornment it is quite exceptional.

Mingled with the abundance of Italian marbles and sculptural decoration which form part of the internal structure, are paintings and furnishings which were contributed by many of the leading artists and craftsmen of the day. The interior is an exposition of Sedding's creed that a church should be 'wrought and painted over with everything that has life and beauty'. The great east window with its 48 small individual panels, each containing a saint, was designed by Burne-Jones with the help of William Morris. The altar rails, the grille behind the side altar and the black and gold railings outside the church are all by Henry Wilson, Sedding's successor, who continued the embellishment of Holy Trinity after the architect's death in 1891. Sir John Betjeman, who was a worshipper here, was moved to write these lines:

Bronze triptych doors unswing!
Wait, restive heart, wait, rounded lips, to pray,
'Mid beaten copper interset with gems,
Behold! Behold! your King.

FAR LEFT The Brompton Oratory

BELOW LEFT Holy Trinity, Sloane Street

BELOW St Augustine's, Queen's Gate

ST AUGUSTINE'S, QUEEN'S GATE
Queen's Gate (between Manson Place and Harrington Road), SW7
(William Butterfield, 1870-6)

Although the building of St Augustine's was not started until 1870, the followers of the Rev. R. R. Chope, a High Church curate of Holy Trinity, Brompton, had been campaigning for five years for a new church of which he should be the first incumbent. Permission was granted in 1869 by the newly appointed Bishop of London, and William Butterfield was offered the assignment.

Like his All Saints, Margaret Street, this church, too, is an affirmation of his deep religious commitment. But architecturally there are differences. All Saints suggests great height, St Augustine's conveys a sense of breadth. It stands, facing west, slightly at an angle to the street front, its strange, tall-windowed façade composed of alternate bands of red and yellow brick and Bath stone. It is surmounted by a small belfry instead of a tower.

Inside, a great wide nave leads into a chancel of the same width and height, the transition marked by a broad arch. In its early days the church fairly blazed with colour, brilliant decoration mingling with multi-coloured marble and alabaster, tiles and wall murals. In the 1920s the murals were covered up and the decoration shrouded in whitewash as a background for gilded furnishings by Martin Travers, the outstanding one being the reredos, gilded and lacquered, unmistakably of the early twentieth century, which earned for the church the nickname 'the Essoldo', Queen's Gate. But fortunately another swing of fashion has renewed Butterfield's colours and restored St Augustine's to its former glory. The font, pulpit and lectern we all designed by Butterfield and are contemporary with the church.

—◆—

ST BARNABAS'S, ADDISON ROAD, W14
(Lewis Vulliamy, 1827-9)

St Barnabas's, largely funded by the 1818 Commission, was built in 1827–9 by Lewis Vulliamy for the inhabitants of West Kensington whose parish church of St Mary Abbots was too far away to reach on foot. Based on the late Perpendicular design of King's College Chapel, Cambridge, which was extremely popular at the time, the church is constructed in stock brick with octagonal turrets

RIGHT St Augustine's, Queen's Gate

BELOW St Barnabas's, Addison Road

at the corners, a western porch and plenty of Gothic tracery. The proportions of the interior are harmonious, with galleries on three sides resting on cast-iron columns. The chancel, added in 1860 by Thomas Johnson and reconstructed in 1909 by T. G. Jackson, is entered through an arch which is flanked on either side by two openwork traceried bays. The unusually large crypt is the head-quarters of the London Boy Singers, a choir formed in 1961 under the patronage of Benjamin Britten. It was in this church that T. S. Eliot married his second wife in 1957.

◆

ST COLUMBA'S CHURCH OF SCOTLAND
Pont Street, SW1
(Edward Maufe, 1950-55)

The Victorian church which stood formerly on this site had been built in 1883–4 to provide a central place of worship in London for Scottish Presbyterians. It was destroyed by a bomb in 1941, and the present church, designed by Sir Edward Maufe, was erected in its place during the 1950s.

RIGHT St Luke's, Chelsea

BELOW St Columba's Church of Scotland

ST LUKE'S, CHELSEA
Sydney Street, SW3
(James Savage, 1820-24)

A new parish church to serve the expanding district of Chelsea was authorised by Act of Parliament in 1819, and James Savage was chosen to design it. It has been described by Charles Eastlake, the learned Victorian authority on architecture, as 'the earliest groined church of the modern revivial'. Eastlake also felt that, in its very precision of Gothic detail, it failed to capture the true spirit of a medieval church. None the less, St Luke's is an extremely impressive building, standing surrounded by open spaces and built entirely of stone (at the enormous cost of £40,000). The four-pinnacled tower on the west front rises 142 feet high and the entrance through it is flanked on either side by two bays, all together forming an open porch across the whole façade. The vaults outside are heavily buttressed. The interior is equally imposing with its lofty stone nave, the triforium and clerestory both extending into the chancel. Wooden galleries hang between slender piers, and there is a large seven-light window with modern stained glass by Hugh Easton at the east end. Below it, and contemporary with the church, is a dramatic scene of the 'Descent from the Cross' painted by James Northcote. The west end is panelled in stone. The organ casing bears the Royal Arms of George IV. The instrument, which is very fine, dates from 1824 but was rebuilt in 1932 by John Compton. Early this century it was played by John Ireland, who was organist here between 1904–26.

It was in this church that the ill-starred marriage of Charles Dickens and Catherine Hogarth took place in 1836. Charles Kingsley was curate here in the 1830s. A lengthy restoration of the church began in 1985.

◆

ST MARY ABBOTS
Church Street, Kensington, W8
(George Gilbert Scott, 1869-79)

St Mary Abbots was originally attached to the Abbey of Abingdon. The early church was rebuilt in 1370 and again in the 1690s when a pew was reserved for royalty. William III and Mary used

ABOVE *St Mary Abbots*

RIGHT *St Mary's, Cadogan Street*

to attend services here as there was then no chapel at Kensington Palace. The King's gift of a pulpit is still in the present church, but the church itself was rebuilt between 1869–79. The architect was George Gilbert Scott and St Mary's is his last but one London church. It is very large with a towering steeple, 278 feet high. The outside is faced with Kentish ragstone and it is built in the style of the late thirteenth century. This is repeated in the interior, which is faced with stone. The columns in the chancel are formed of Irish marble. Of the monuments, the most noteworthy is the grand memorial erected in 1721 to the 7th Earl of Warwick.

The cloistered walk (built 1890) which leads to the church also gives access to the garden which lies behind it. Overlooking it are the painted stone figures of two charity children. These used to stand on the front of the old parish school built by Hawksmoor and demolished in the nineteenth century.

◆

ST MARY'S, CADOGAN STREET
Cadogan Street, SW3
(J. F. Bentley, 1877-82)

During the Napoleonic wars an emigré priest, the Abbé Voyaux de Franous, established a small chapel here for the use of French prisoners-of-war lodged in the locality. St Mary's, which replaced the chapel, was built between 1877–82. The austere design is by J. F. Bentley in the Early English manner. There were alterations in the 1970s when the sanctuary was rearranged to enable the priest to face the congregation while celebrating Mass. The rector at that time was Canon John Longstaff, a descendant of St Thomas More.

◆

Also of interest in Kensington and Chelsea: the recently repaired All Saints, Talbot Road, W11 by William White (1852–5); St Cuthbert's, Philbeach Gardens, SW5 (1884–7) by Roumieu and Gough with magnificent furnishings, some by William Bainbridge Reynolds; and St Stephen's, Gloucester road, SW7 by G. F. Bodley (1866–7) where T. S. Eliot was churchwarden for 25 years.

RICHMOND

◆

ALL HALLOWS, NORTH TWICKENHAM
Chertsey Road, Twickenham, Middlesex
(Wren Tower, 1686-94)

The white, stone tower, balustraded with an arcade of pierced spandrels, which stands by the modern brick church of All Hallows, is not indigenous. It used to belong to the Wren church of All Hallows, Lombard Street which became unsafe in the late 1930s and was pulled down. At its demise, the tower, porch and furnishings were transplanted to Twickenham where, although at variance with their latterday surroundings, they can at least be seen in a better light than formerly.

Immediately within the tower is the old porch, a legacy from the Priory of St John, Clerkenwell, which is gruesomely embellished with skulls, skel-

etons and other relics. The interior of the new church, in itself unremarkable, is distinguished by its splendid seventeenth- and eighteenth-century furnishings: doorcases, pews, pulpit, font, organ and chandeliers are among the fittings. But the greatest treasure is the reredos, richly carved, much pedimented and overflowing with classical motifs.

◆

ST ANNE'S, KEW GREEN
Kew, Surrey (1710-14)

The area around Kew Green had, from its proximity to Richmond Palace, long been associated with royalty, and it was Queen Anne who gave the site on which the church, linked with her name, still stands. It was consecrated in 1714, and enlarged around 1770, mainly at the expense of George III, who was taking possession of Kew Palace at the time. In 1836 his son, William IV, provided 200 free seats on the north side of the church; and it was in St Anne's, thirty years later, that Princess Mary of Cambridge was married to the Duke of Teck.

The church, in its present form, dates mainly from the nineteenth century when there were a number of additions, including a portico and bell-turret. The interior is long, with a vaulted ceiling and timber columns. Thomas Gainsborough is buried in the churchyard.

◆

ST MARY'S, BARNES
Church Road, SW13

On 8 June 1978 the medieval parish church of St Mary was largely destroyed by fire. The present church, designed by Edward Cullinan, combines a substantial part of the old building with a completely new one. The Tudor tower had been left standing, together with parts of the medieval nave and the twelfth-century Langton Chapel. These, meticulously restored, form one part of the newly constructed church while the modern additions are radically different, although wherever possible

LEFT All Hallows, North Twickenham

RIGHT St Mary's, Barnes

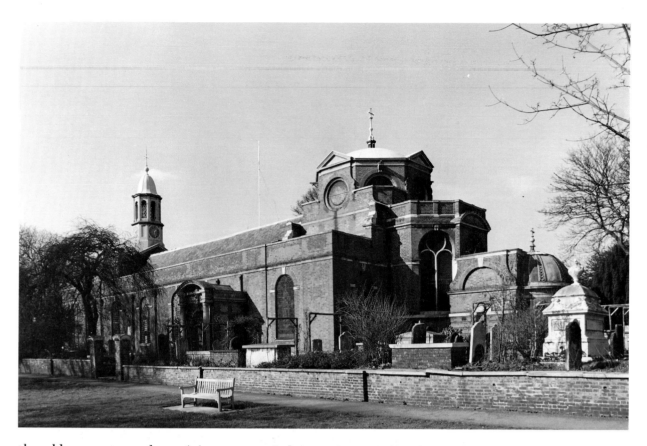

the old masonry and surviving stone window mouldings have been introduced into the new walls. The dominating feature of the new exterior is the beautiful red-orange roof of hand-made clay tiles. It appears to float over the whole building, dipping nearly to the ground over the new transept, and is supported inside by a timber struc-

St Anne's, Kew Green

ture of ingenious design and great complexity, which forms part of the decoration of the interior. This is in white-washed brick, having modern furnishings in keeping with the simplicity of the new structure.

◆

EAST LONDON

NEWHAM

ST MARY MAGDALENE, EAST HAM
High Street South, E6

ABOVE St Mary Magdalene

St Mary Magdalene, built in about 1130 and still in use as a parish church, is almost unchanged in appearance since its foundation. The tower was added in the sixteenth century, but other additions and alterations have been minor. The semicircular arch at the entrance to the apse is Norman; so is the timbered roof above it, held together by wooden pegs; and so is the doorway at the west end. A double piscina to the south-east of the sanctuary dates from the thirteenth century, and later furnishings include a 1639 font and churchwardens' prickers of 1805, used to prod the somnolent to attention during the sermon. St Mary Magdalene is thought to have the largest churchyard in England. Today, the nine acres in which the church stands have been transformed into a nature reserve by the Passmore Edwards Museum.

◆

TOWER HAMLETS

◆

ALL SAINTS, POPLAR
East India Dock Road, E15
(Charles Hollis, 1821-3)

The church for the brand new parish of Poplar-and-Blackwall was consecrated in 1823. It had been built by Charles Hollis with funds subscribed by the inhabitants. It is a large handsome church in Portland stone, rectangular in shape, having a massive projecting portico of Ionic columns inspired by an Athenian temple. This is flanked on either side by similar columned porches, the southern one now containing a chapel, the northern one a vestry. There are two tiers of windows to the side walls, the upper ones being arched. The tower rising centrally behind the portico is reminiscent of steeples by Wren and Gibbs. The first stage is square with attached columns, a small clock stage succeeds it, and the third stage, showing detached columns, is crowned by an obelisk. The interior was remodelled in the 1950s by Cecil Brown in the manner of the eighteenth century. It contains a striking *baldacchino* over the altar and an imposing west gallery which bears the Royal Arms and contains the organ.

An epitaph in the graveyard commemorates John Wild Bennett, a brass worker who was buried here in 1838, with these words: 'Like a worn out type he's returned to the Founder to be recast in a better and more perfect mould'.

◆

CHRIST CHURCH, SPITALFIELDS
Commercial Street by Fournier Street, E1
(Nicholas Hawksmoor, 1714-15)

From 1197 until the sixteenth century, the site of Spital Square was occupied by the Priory of St Mary Spittle. a hospice which used to provide lodging for poor travellers. The Spital Cross, the outdoor pulpit in the Priory grounds from which the Easter sermons (Spital Sermons) were preached, survived the Dissolution of the Monasteries and remained in use until 1642. At that

time there were already a few silk workers living in the area, but by the end of the seventeenth century their numbers had been greatly increased

Christ Church, Spitalfields

by an influx of Huguenot refugees attracted to Spitalfields by the already existing silk industry. In their wake followed prosperity, and under the Fifty New Churches Act, Nicholas Hawksmoor was invited to design a church to serve their community.

Of Hawksmoor's six London churches, Christ Church has often been acclaimed the finest. But its construction was dogged by recurring financial crises and, although the foundations were laid in 1715, it was not consecrated until 1729. The exterior is magnificent in stone. It is a long, rectangular building with monumental walls, fronted by a vast portico of four Tuscan columns with a semi-circular arch in the middle. The width of the portico is carried upwards by the square buttresses of the tower, which gives way to a soaring temple,

more Gothic than Classical in feeling, which was simplified in an early nineteenth-century restoration after a fire. The interior, described by Sir John Betjeman as 'massive, simple and gigantic', is planned around a central square with a central cross axis. There is a flat coffered ceiling, and high arcades of slender columns and round arches lead to the east end, where an architrave, bearing the Royal Arms in Coade stone and spanning the nave with the support of two additional columns in the middle, forms the entrance to the chancel. A Venetian window completes the vista to the east, and to the west a magnificent organ, the largest

ABOVE Christ Church, Spitalfields

LEFT All Saints, Poplar

in England at the time, carried on a gallery with fluted mahogany pillars takes up the view.

The Industrial Revolution brought death to the hand silkweaving trade and penury to Spitalfields. Such was the poverty throughout the nineteenth century that, although some repairs and alterations to the church were carried out, hardly any money could be spared, and in this century Christ Church had deteriorated to such an extent that by 1958 it was considered dangerous and was closed for public worship.

Plans to demolish it and sell the site were being considered; but when the news got out the proposal was quashed and an organisation, the Friends of Christ Church Spitalfields, was formed subsequently for its preservation. As a result this great architectural work was being restored in 1987.

ST ANNE'S, LIMEHOUSE
Commercial Road at West India Dock Road, E14 (Nicholas Hawksmoor, 1714-24)

St Anne's, one of the Fifty New Churches designed for the suburbs of London, was built in open fields immediately to the north of the riverside colony of Limehouse, for years a shipbuilding settlement. Its design has often been likened to the spread of sails on a square-rigged ship, and its tower used to be a nautical landmark for vessels sailing up Limehouse Reach. It was the first of Nicholas Hawksmoor's three magnificent Stepney churches. After the consecration, which was delayed until 1729 because of problems in raising the stipend for a rector, 'the bishope drank a little hot wine,' a parishioner recorded, 'and took a bitt of the sweetmeats, and then the clergy and the laity scrambled for the rest.' St Anne's was gutted by fire on Good Friday 1850, and was not immediately rebuilt as the two nonconformist church-wardens would not sanction the collection of the repair money by a church rate. However, voluntary contributions, together with some insurance cover which they had had the fore-

thought to provide, produced sufficient funds for a restoration in 1851-3 by Philip Hardwick and John Morris. There were further renovations by Sir Arthur Blomfield in 1891, but by the 1970s the church was again in very poor repair. However, since 1981 it has been the subject of a major restoration which is to extend until 1990, and much has already been achieved.

Standing in a very large open churchyard, St Anne's presents an awe-inspiring exterior, stone-faced and built in Hawksmoor's Roman style. The north and south walls are long and plain, the windows round-headed. There is a semi-circular porch at the west end above which a broad tower rises to a complex top terminating in four little square spires. The flat pedimented east end is flanked by turrets. The interior has a square centre with columns arranged to create a Greek cross effect. There are galleries on three sides, and the great circular ceiling hanging above the nave is reflected in the rounded arch over the chancel, where the large east window, made of coloured enamel on white glass, acts as the reredos. The 1853 pulpit with pedestal and staircase is a magnificent piece by the Victorian woodcarver, W. Gibbs Rogers; and the superb 3-manual organ in the west gallery, built by Gray and Davison for the Great Exhibition of 1851 and installed here afterwards, has hardly been altered.

It is reassuring to see (in 1987) in what good condition the interior of the church seems to be, although it is to be repaired and redecorated between 1988–90. St Anne's is normally closed except for services.

◆

ST DUNSTAN'S, STEPNEY
Stepney High Street, E1

Some time late in the tenth century, a small Saxon church known as All Saints was enlarged or rebuilt by Dunstan, Bishop of London from 959–961 AD. The dedication to him was made after his canonisation in 1029. In the Middle Ages the district of Stepney, although large, was virtually open country and the little church of St Dunstan sufficed the needs of the sparsely populated parish. By the end of the fifteenth century, however, the number of inhabitants had increased and the present church dates mainly from an enlargement and rebuilding of that time, although the chancel is a survival from the late thirteenth century.

The exterior, rectangular and battlemented, is constructed in Kentish ragstone with a square tower, pinnacled at each corner. Frequent alterations were carried out in the eighteenth and nineteenth centuries. Stucco, applied in 1767, was removed in 1806; porches and an octagonal vestry were added in Victorian times; and the exterior was refaced in ragstone in 1871–2. Severe damage caused by a fire in 1901 was repaired, largely through the generosity of the Charrington family whose brewery was nearby, and there was further restoration after the Second World War.

The interior is long and low, the nave stretching without interruption into the chancel where, on the south-east wall, is a triple sedilia dating from the thirteenth century. Also in the chancel is a fourteenth-century depiction of the Annunciation. The colours of the modern east window by Hugh Easton make a curious contrast with the ancient rood above the altar. Placed in the tower in 1663 is a stone, taken from the walls of Carthage, with the words 'Time consumes all; it spareth none'.

Standing in its large open churchyard, St Dunstan's, despite much restoration, still manages to retain something of its medieval character. John

LEFT St Anne's, Limehouse

BELOW St Dunstan's, Stepney

Colet, who founded St Paul's School, was vicar here in 1485. His father, Sir Henry Colet, was buried in the church in 1510.

◆

ST GEORGE'S-IN-THE-EAST
Cannon Street Road, at the Highway, E1
(Nicholas Hawksmoor, 1715-23)

St George's, standing in a large walled churchyard, is one of three splendid churches built in Stepney by Nicholas Hawksmoor under the 1711 Act, and was designed to provide a place of worship for the inhabitants of Upper Wapping. The project was beset with financial difficulties, and the new church was not consecrated until 1729. It was to become notorious in the next century. In 1842, the new incumbent, Bryan King, following the precepts of Bishop Blomfield, initiated a moderate form of High Church ritual, a practice which brought him into violent conflict with the succeeding Bishop of London, A.C. Tait, who had been born a Presbyterian. Despite King's opposition, Tait licensed the appointment of Hugh Allen, a militant Low Churchman, as afternoon lecturer at St George's, and Allen set about the task of baiting the rector with unseemly enthusiasm. Services were disrupted, disgraceful scenes

made a magnificent ruin.' In 1963 a new church, invisible from outside, was set up within the Hawksmoor shell. It does not attempt to recreate the old interior, but it is pleasant and practicable. The furnishings are all new except for the plasterwork of the apse and the restored mosaics of 1880.

◆

ST JOHN ON BETHNAL GREEN
Cambridge Heath Road, E2
(John Soane, 1825-8)

St John's, built by the so-called Waterloo Commission between 1825–8, is the second of Sir John Soane's London churches. The west front shows three large bays divided by pilasters, the central bay going up to an attic from which rises a low

and rioting ensued, and for six weeks, in 1859, the church was closed for a truce. Even when it reopened, Bishop Tait refused to support the Rector, the Rector refused to abandon his High Church practices, and the battle continued until finally, his health shattered, King was persuaded to hand over to a locum. Many years later, a large mosaic 'Crucifixion' was placed over the altar by the vestry in a gesture of opposition to King's successor. It remains there to this day.

The exterior of Hawksmoor's monumental church is faced with Portland stone, and its noble proportions, while essentially plain, are enhanced by emphatic details such as the huge keystone above some of the side doors and windows. The latter are deeply recessed, and the roof sports a profusion of turrets crowned with cupolas. The tower, supported by grooved piers, is 160 feet high. It is topped by a highly original open octagonal lantern. The interior was gutted during the Second World War, and Canon Basil Clarke, in his book *Parish Churches of London*, records a visit to St George's while still in its derelict state: 'Though it was sad to see the church in its state of dereliction, there was no denying that Hawksmoor's walls

ABOVE St John on Bethnal Green

ABOVE LEFT St George's-in-the-East

RIGHT St Anne's, Limehouse

squat tower. This is flanked at each corner by two detached pillars and is topped by an incongruous little circular cupola. The interior was severely damaged by fire in 1870, and the subsequent Victorian re-modelling has completely altered the original design. There is now a hammerbeam roof, and the windows are filled with inappropriate tracery. Only the vestibule, offering a dramatic vista through the arches opening to the basement under the tower, is still Soane's own work.

The fine site on which the church stands has been blighted by the main railway line, which cuts across its western façade.

◆

ST MARY'S, STRATFORD LE BOW
Bow Road, Poplar, E3

The church was built as a chapel of ease to Stepney Parish Church in 1311, but it was not made parochial until 1719 when it took its dedication. The surname 'Bow' derives from the arches of the nearby bridge over the River Lea. Although much of the ancient fabric still remains, the church has been heavily restored over the centuries, most recently by Sir Albert Richardson after the Second

World War when St Mary's was severely damaged.

The body of the church is constructed in ragstone rubble, but the top of the tower has been renewed in brick. Inside it is long and narrow with irregularly bayed arcades. The ceiling is high showing pale oak rafters and the walls are simply white-washed. There are a few interesting seventeenth- and eighteenth-century monuments and an early fifteenth-century font.

◆

ST NICHOLAS'S, DEPTFORD
Deptford Green, SE8
(Charley Stanton, 1679)

The medieval church of St Nicholas, which in the late seventeenth century still served the parish of Deptford, a centre of shipbuilding since Tudor times, was found to be too small for the increasing population of the area. It was demolished and reconstructed in 1697 by the builder, Charley Stanton, who kept the old, early sixteenth-century

LEFT St Mary's, Stratford le Bow

BELOW St Nicholas's, Deptford

on the east wall, and a tablet on the west wall records the death of Christopher Marlowe, the Elizabethan dramatist, killed in 1593 in a tavern brawl.

St Nicholas's is approached through a gate flanked by pillars each crowned by a gruesome death's-head skull. It stands in a quiet backwater, surrounded by a leafy walled churchyard.

It is closed except on Friday and for services.

◆

ST PAUL'S, SHADWELL
The Highway, E1
(John Walters, 1817-20)

St Paul's was built as a chapel of ease to St Dunstan's, Stepney in 1656, and became parochial in 1669. The present church, designed by John Walters and built in 1817–20, stands in a secluded churchyard near the river. It is constructed in brick with a double row of rectangular windows

tower. This was soon afterwards considered dangerous, but proposals for building another church, or just rebuilding the steeple, came to nothing as the Fifty New Churches Commission refused any financial assistance. According to a stone on the south side, the building 'was Oblig'd to be supported by a thorough repair and strap'd with Iron. The Charge being near £400 AD 1716'. Surprisingly, this repair kept the church intact until the Second World War when it was gutted.

An admirable post-war restoration by Thomas F. Ford and Partners reduced its size by cutting off the eastern bay to produce a church hall and other amenities, and St Nicholas was reopened in 1958.

The body of the church is constructed in dark red brick, quite plain with round-headed windows, in a style deriving from Wren. The transepts are marked by Dutch gables. The tower is in ragstone in marked contrast to the brick. The restored interior is light with large areas of clear glass and has some original furnishings which include the pulpit, a magnificent piece with a staircase of twisted balusters, and reredos containing some notable carvings of Ezekiel and the Valley of Bones. A painting of Queen Anne by Kneller hangs

LEFT St Nicholas's, Deptford

ABOVE Reredos detail, St Nicholas's, Deptford

RIGHT St Paul's, Shadwell

and a stuccoed front with pilasters. The steeple, reminiscent of St Leonard's, Shoredith, has a circular upper stage with columns and a slender obelisk. The galleried interior, rearranged by Butterfield in 1848, has a shallow saucer dome and contains the original seventeenth-century font and pot-bellied pulpit.

Situated in what was once an almost exclusively nautical area, St Paul's was sometimes known as The Church of the Sea Captains. Between 1730 and 1790 more than 175 names of naval commanders and their wives appear in the register.

◆

SOUTH LONDON

CROYDON

ALL SAINTS, UPPER NORWOOD
Beulah Hill, SE19
(James Savage, 1827-9)

All Saints, built as a chapel of ease to Croydon parish church by James Savage in 1827–9, started as a simple rectangle with galleries and box pews. The tower was added in 1841, and the Victorian chancel twenty years later. All Saints is mentioned by Charles Dickens in *David Copperfield*, and was painted by Pissarro during his stay in Palace Road at the time of the Franco-Prussian War.

ST JOHN THE EVANGELIST, UPPER NORWOOD
Sylvan Road, SE19
(J. L. Pearson, 1878-87)

St John's is a splendid example of the work of J. L. Pearson who was commissioned to build the church through the efforts of the Rev. W. F. Bateman whose first church in the parish, where he was to remain for 26 years, was a small building of iron. Pearson's tall lancets and high-pitched roof are a perfect setting for his accomplished Early English style.

LEFT All Saints, Upper Norwood

BELOW St John the Evangelist, Upper Norwood

GREENWICH

GREENWICH ROYAL HOSPITAL CHAPEL
Greenwich, SE10
(James 'Athenian' Stuart and
William Newton, 1779-89)

The buildings of the Royal Naval Hospital (now the Royal Naval College and Maritime Museum) evolved from, and stand on the site of, the former royal palace at Greenwich. Inigo Jones, John Webb, Christopher Wren, Nicholas Hawksmoor, John Vanbrugh and James Stuart all had a hand in them.

The former Queen's House, designed by Inigo Jones and completed for Henrietta Maria in 1640, formed the central point of the Royal Naval Hospital which was founded for naval pensioners in the 1690s. This Hospital, designed by Wren and worked on by several others, was eventually finished by Thomas Ripley in 1752. Not long after, its chapel was severely damaged by fire (1779) and

was rebuilt by James 'Athenian' Stuart, most of the detailed work being carried out by his Clerk of Works, William Newton.

Designed in the neo-Grecian manner, the chapel is extremely well preserved. It is entered through an octagonal vestibule containing four large statues, in Coade stone, featuring Faith, Hope, Charity and Humility by Benjamin West, who also executed the vast dark painting of St Paul and the Viper which hangs over the gilt stone and marble altar at the east end of the interior. The pulpit, circular in shape and carved in red limewood, is an exceptionally fine furnishing; and there is a proliferation of sea emblems displayed in the decoration, which was carefully renewed in 1955.

The Royal Hospital Chapel belongs today to the Royal Naval College, which took over in 1879 when the pensioners moved out.

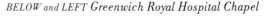

BELOW and LEFT Greenwich Royal Hospital Chapel

WHOEVER SHALL GIVE TO DRINK
UNTO ONE OF THESE LITTLE ONES
A CUP OF COLD WATER ONLY IN
THE NAME OF A DISCIPLE VERILY
I SAY UNTO YOU, HE SHALL IN
NO WISE LOSE HIS REWARD

ST ALFEGE'S, GREENWICH
Greenwich Church Street, SE10
(Nicholas Hawksmoor, 1714-18;
Tower, John James, 1730)

The present church of St Alfege is probably the third to stand on ground hallowed by the martyrdom of St Alfege, Archbishop of Canterbury who, taken hostage by Danish invaders at the sack of Canterbury in 1011, forbade his people to ransom him and was murdered here in Greenwich in the following year by his captors.

The first church is thought to have been built soon after, and was replaced by another in the late thirteenth century. This had its heyday in the time of the Tudors when the court was frequently lodged at Greenwich Palace. John Morton, later Cardinal and Chancellor of England, was vicar here from 1444 to 1454. In 1491, Henry VIII was baptized here, and here, too, his sister Mary married the Duke of Suffolk in 1514. Samuel Pepys records a visit to the church in 1661: 'By coach to Greenwich church, where a good sermon, a fine church, and a great company of handsome women.'

In 1710, the roof of the old church collapsed and the parish petitioned for a new church. The petition was favourably considered, and St Alfege's was the first church to be completed under the 1711 Act. However, parish opposition to the installation of a Royal Pew delayed consecration until 1718 when the pew was finally set in place. The usual money shortages prevented the erection of Hawksmoor's tower, and in the end the lower part of the old tower (dating from a rebuilding of 1617) was retained, faced in stone and extended by John James who completed it in 1730. A few repairs were carried out in Victorian times, and there was an excellent restoration under Sir Albert Richardson following bomb damage in 1941.

St Alfege's is shaped like a temple, Roman in feeling, with central projecting vestibules on the north and south sides. The main façade is to the east and contains an enormous recessed portico with a large plain pediment. At each corner, and at each end of the ridge of the roof, there is a huge stone urn. The James tower at the west end seems quite irrelevant to the rest of the building, and is disappointingly out of keeping with the grandeur

ABOVE RIGHT St Alfege's, Greenwich

LEFT Statue by Benjamin West, Greenwich Royal Hospital Chapel

of the overall design. Inside, a great oval ceiling, suspended by tie beams, embraces the whole rectangular space, and at the east end, well below ceiling level, a depressed half-dome is set under the apse. Low galleries on three sides supported on little wooden posts suggest a proximity to the floor rather than a half-way stage to the roof. The pilasters at the east end, and the apse, painted originally by Sir James Thornhill in *trompe-l'oeil*, were faithfully repainted by Glyn Jones in 1952; and several windows – including the eastern one – were installed by F. H. Spear in the following year. Much of the former wood carving was by Grinling Gibbons, but most of it was destroyed during the war and only a little of his work remains in the posts under the galleries and the Beasts on the Royal Pew. All the surviving woodwork has been restored to its original shade of rich gold, and the new pulpit, a notable although simplified copy of the former Wren furnishing, is in matching tones. The wrought-iron work of the altar rails and gallery rails to the north and south of the altar are original, their design being ascribed to Jean Tijou. A 1552 organ, in use until 1910, the console of which is in a glass case in the south-west corner of the present church, is thought to have been used by Thomas Tallis who was buried here in 1585. A window in the south aisle commemorates him.

St Peter's, which used to stand nearby, was destroyed in the Second World War, and its parish is united with that of St Alfege.

◆

ST LUKE'S, CHARLTON VILLAGE, SE7 (c. 1630)

There is mention of a church here in 1077, but little is known about it except that it belonged to the Abbey of Bermondsey. In 1607 it was acquired by Sir Adam Newton, the owner of nearby Charlton House, at whose expense it was rebuilt in about 1630. The present church dates from then, and despite subsequent alterations and additions, its charming village appearance has hardly changed. It is built in brick, probably incorporating parts of the former walls, with a square, embattled tower, the clasping buttresses of which terminate in small turrets. The windows are pointed except for an eighteenth-century round

one, and there is a simple Dutch-gabled south porch. The white-washed interior is low and modest, with a two bay nave separated from the north aisle by two round-headed arches and one square pier. There is a good scattering of monuments, including a particularly fine one to Sir Adam and Lady Newton. On the west wall of the north aisle is a tablet, with a portrait bust above, to Spencer Perceval who was assassinated in the House of Commons in 1812. In the rector's vault lies another victim of assassination, Charles Edward Drummond, brother of the then rector, killed by a maniac in mistake for Sir Robert Peel.

Because St Luke's was a landmark from the Thames and was used as a navigational aid in the past, it is authorised on St George's and St Luke's Days to fly the British Ensign from a flagpole outside. The church is normally locked except for services.

◆

ST MARY MAGDALENE, WOOLWICH
St Mary's Street, SE18 (1727-39)

There has been a church here since about 1100. In the early eighteenth century the medieval structure was threatened with subsidence, the cliff site on which it stood having been undermined by excavation of sand for ballast. The parishioners were granted money from the Fifty New Churches Commission to rebuild, and a new church was erected on a safer site slightly to the south of the old one, which remained standing for some years. It is not known who designed it, but the foundations were laid by Matthew Spray, a Deptford bricklayer, 'under the supervision of two gentlemen'. Because of financial difficulties the tower was not completed until 1739.

It is a brick building with two-storeyed arched windows and a west tower. The interior is of five bays with galleries resting on octagonal columns. The east gallery has been removed and the others are now shut off from the church. The chancel, organ chamber and vestry, which were added by John Oldrid Scott in 1894, blend agreeably with the overall eighteenth-century style. In the Lady Chapel to the right is an interesting altarpiece,

LEFT St Luke's, Charlton Village

RIGHT St Mary Magdalene, Woolwich

moved from the old east end, which displays some very fine carving. The monuments in and around the church testify to long associations with the Army and Navy.

ST NICHOLAS'S, PLUMSTEAD
Plumstead High Street, SE18

The church of St Nicholas Plumstead has its origins in the twelfth century when it was built to serve a small community of fruit growers. In the seventeenth century it was rescued from a state of decay by John Gossage, a wealthy farmer, after it had been 'above 20 years lying waste and ruinous'. The substantial, dark red brick tower, with clasping buttresses rising into battlemented turrets, dates from the 1662–4 rebuilding. By 1800, however, the church was again open to the skies with trees growing in the aisles. A restoration in

1818 was followed by another in 1867–8 by C. H. Cooke, and there was a considerable enlargement in 1907–8. St Nicholas's was gutted in the Second World War, repaired by F. Ford & Partners and reopened in 1959.

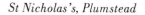

Also of interest in Greenwich: St Michael and All Angels, Blackheath Park, a Gothic Revival Church by George Smith (1830).

St Nicholas's, Plumstead

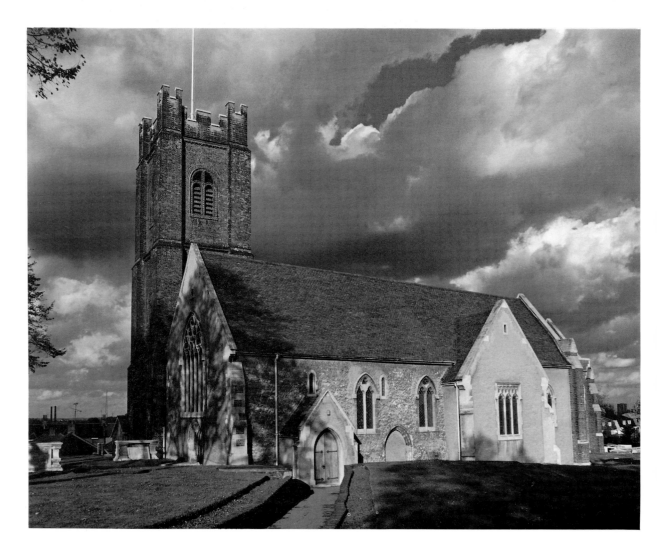

LAMBETH

All Saints, West Dulwich

ALL SAINTS, WEST DULWICH
Rosendale Road, SE21
(G. H. Fellowes Prynne, 1888-91)

All Saints, a massive red-brick structure, stands
on a steep slope dominating Rosendale Road. The
site was the gift of Dulwich College, and the architect, G. H. Fellowes Prynne, still a young man,
produced an unusual design for a suburban parish
church. The wide nave, characteristic of the thirteenth century, is joined to the chancel, which is
in the style of the fourteenth century, by a narrow,
canted bay, which has a traceried stone screen
filling the whole of the chancel arch. There are
tall, thin windows to the apse, around which are
ambulatories. There are also ambulatories around
the apse to the Lady Chapel at the north side.
Because of the slope, the body of the church containing the vestries lies on a lower level. Only a
modest little tower, erected in 1952 by J. B. S.
Comper, stands in place of the tall one originally
intended, and the west end of the church remains
unfinished to this day.

HOLY TRINITY, CLAPHAM
Clapham Common (North Side), SW4
(Kenton Couse, 1774-6)

The original parish church, dedicated to St Mary,
had been in existence since the twelfth century
and was beyond repair by the 1750s. It was then
agreed not to spend any more money on the old
building, but to replace it with a new church. The
scheme hung fire, and it was not until 1775 that
Holy Trinity Church was built, in a charming new
setting on the north side of the Common, to serve
the increasing population in the parish.

The architect was Kenton Couse, a pupil of
Henry Flitcroft, and the building is a simple rectangle in brick with stone quoins. The windows
are round-headed and there is a stone turret
crowned by a large octagonal domed cupola. A
Doric colonnade by Francis Hurlbatt replaced the
original pedimented west porch in 1812. The
interior is plain; the pews were cut down and the

Holy Trinity, Clapham

Johnson, who worshipped there when staying with his friends, the Thrales. When Henry Thrale died, his widow married Piozzi and on her departure from the neighbourhood, Dr Johnson took his leave of St Leonard's church with a kiss. The Latin epitaphs he wrote on Mrs Thrale's mother and on Henry Thrale were reinstated in the new church, where they can be seen at the end of the north aisle. There are a large number of monuments, including a magnificent memorial to John Howland who died in 1686. The chancel was added in 1862 by William Dyce, the painter, who was a churchwarden here and is commemorated by a fine brass.

◆

St Leonard's, Streatham

pulpit lowered in Victorian times and the chancel, which replaced the apse in 1902, is by A. Beresford Pite. The church was restored after the Second World War by Thomas Ford.

It is interesting for its past associations with the Evangelical Movement whose local members (known as the Clapham Sect) are commemorated by a plaque on the south side of the church. They include Zachary Macaulay, Granville Sharp, Henry and John Thornton, John Venn and William Wilberforce.

◆

ST LEONARD'S, STREATHAM
Streatham High Road, SW16
(Joseph Parkinson, 1831)

Although St Leonard's, Streatham is one of the oldest places of worship in London, the present church dates only from 1831 and is an amalgam of later additions and reconstructions, the last in 1975 after a calamitous fire. The church it replaced was notable for its association with Samuel

ST MARY-AT-LAMBETH
Lambeth Palace Road, SE1
(Philip Hardwick, 1851-2)

Even before the foundation (around 1200) of Lambeth Palace, the official residence of the Archbishops of Canterbury, there was a parish church at Lambeth which is recorded in Domesday Book. It was rebuilt four times during its early history, and by the mid-nineteenth century was again beyond repair. Philip Hardwick, commissioned to design a new church, retained the fourteenth-century tower and, keeping to the outline of the old foundations, reconstructed St Mary's in a fourteenth-century style reproducing, as closely as possible, the details of the former church. During the Second World War it was badly damaged and, although afterwards restored by Godfrey Allen, it was declared redundant in 1972 and thereafter closed, after serving the parish for 900 years.

It remained closed until 1977, when the Tradescant Trust was formed to establish a Museum of Garden History within the church and turn the churchyard into a garden, planted with examples of trees, shrubs and flowers introduced by the Tradescant family, for generations botanists and collectors of rare specimens. The first Tradescant, John, gardener extraordinary to Charles I, was buried in the churchyard in 1638. He lies with his family, surrounded by archbishops early and late, in a fine sculptured mausoleum copied from his monument in the Ashmolean Museum at Oxford, which also contains his Collection of Rarities.

The fabric of the church has been lovingly restored by the Trust, and some of its former fittings remain. At the west end of the south aisle is a font, the only one in London designed for total immersion, which was installed by the Rector in memory of Archbishop Benson some time after his death in 1896. The present stained glass was designed by Francis Stephens in the 1950s to replace what was destroyed in the war. One of the new windows in the south chapel commemorates a pedlar, who gave an acre of land to the parish on condition that he and his dog should be forever depicted in one of the church windows. The existing representation is the fourth since his bequest. In 1910 the acre was sold to the London County Council for £81,000 and County Hall now stands upon the site.

St Mary-at-Lambeth, renewed and restored, together with the Tradescant Garden, are open daily except on Saturdays.

St Mary-at-Lambeth

ST PETER'S, VAUXHALL
Kennington Lane, Vauxhall, SE11
(J. L. Pearson, 1863-4)

The design for St Peter's, when exhibited in 1861 at the Royal Academy, was commended by the *Ecclesiologist* as 'thoroughly satisfactory'. And when the church was completed, it was generally admired as a model of what a town church should be: solid and imposing without, spacious and handsomely furnished within. It is constructed in stock brick, with a little red, and the exterior is notable for its power and simplicity. The west front contains a low three-arched porch beneath two large plate-traceried windows, which are flanked by three massive buttresses. A circular window in the gable above completes the composition, which, although built without the intended steeple, nevertheless dominates the surrounding buildings.

The interior is vaulted throughout in brick, and

St Peter's, Vauxhall

has been preserved from later embellishment or whitewash. All ornamental effects arise from the carving and fittings, which include a notable alabaster and mosaic reredos and a richly carved sedilia. St Peter's is the only Anglo-Catholic church in London which retains, austere and dignified, the sanctuary arrangements of the 1860s. Unfortunaely it is hard to see as it is locked except for services.

◆

Also in Lambeth: C. F. Porden's St Matthew's, Brixton (1822–4), one of the best of the churches built under the 1818 Act, but now turned into a community centre; Christ Church, Streatham, SW2 built in the Italian basilican style in 1840–41 to the designs of John Wild, then aged twenty-nine; St John the Divine, Vassall Road, Kennington, SW9, by G. E. Street (1871–4), restored after severe damage in the Second World War by H. S. Goodhart-Rendel.

◆

LEWISHAM

◆

CHURCH OF THE ASCENSION, BLACKHEATH Dartmouth Row, SE10 (1690-95; rebuilt, 1824)

Originally known as Dartmouth Chapel, the Church of the Ascension was founded as a proprietary chapel by Mrs Susannah Graham at some time between 1690–95 and passed to her nephew, George Legge, later the first Lord Dartmouth. Although initially it was the private chapel of the Dartmouth family, it was used as a chapel of ease for Lewisham at times during the eighteenth and nineteenth centuries when the parish church was out of commission. In 1883 it was made the parish church of a separate ecclesiastical district under

Church of the Ascension, Blackheath

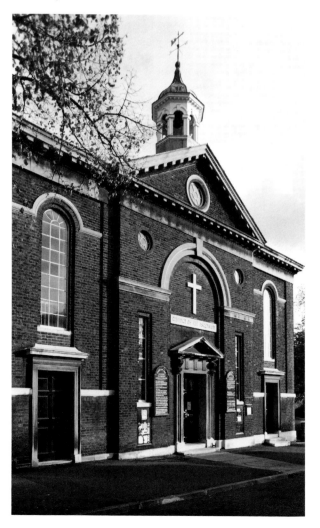

its present dedication.

Although most of the church was rebuilt in 1824, a charming coffered apse framed in coupled columns and piers with gilded capitals survives from the seventeenth-century building. In a restoration by Robert Potter after the Second World War, the north and south galleries were removed, and the western one cut back. It is supported on slender columns of iron encased in plaster and contains a modern Baroque organ. At the same time the ceiling of the nave was rebuilt, and the east end redecorated. Two of the windows contain heraldic glass by Francis Skeat, and the exterior sports a charming little cupola.

◆

ST PAUL'S, DEPTFORD Deptford High Street, at Mary Ann Gardens, SE8 (Thomas Archer, 1712-30)

The parish of St Paul's was formed in 1712 out of the existing parish of St Nicholas to meet the needs of a rapidly expanding population. The new church was designed by Thomas Archer who had studied Italian architecture during his youthful travels on the continent. St Paul's, one of the two churches he built for the Fifty New Churches Commission (the other is St John, Smith Square), testifies to his enthusiasm for the Baroque style.

The huge, white church, set on a stone platform, stands well back at an angle to its large walled churchyard and is approached by a radial staircase of shallow steps. This leads into a great semicircular portico carrying a circular tower, an ingenious solution to an otherwise awkward conjunction, and one that is both structurally convincing and highly original. The curve of the portico is repeated at the east in the rounded line of the apse, above which a pedimented Venetian window follows suit. The porticos on the north and south walls have straight staircases of elaborate design.

Inside the plan is basically square with canted angles behind which lie the vestries. As well as side galleries, there are miniature corner galleries projecting well forward. Huge Corinthian columns define the north and south aisles, and the ceilings are flat with splendid classical plasterwork. Fluted dark wood Corinthian columns support the superb organ gallery at the west end, matching those which carry the four small projecting galleries.

Stretching across the upper section of the apse is a *trompe-l'oeil* painting of crimson curtains, their folds, opening above the altar, their colour and depth making a satisfying contrast with the white walls and ceiling.

St Paul's was spared the heavy hand of Victorian improvement and has recently been restored in a manner that does full justice to this great church.

◆

PREVIOUS PAGES St Paul's, Deptford, exterior and interior

SOUTHWARK

Monument to Thomas Guy, Guy's Hospital Chapel

GUY'S HOSPITAL CHAPEL
St Thomas Street, SE1
(Richard Jupp, 1780)

Although the Hospital was founded in 1722, the Chapel was not built until 1780. It is housed in the block of buildings to the right, as you enter the imposing courtyard which forms the entrance to the Hospital. The interior is very pretty, small and square with galleries on three sides supported on Ionic pillars. The decoration is white with some of the plaster detail picked out in strong blue, in a most attractive combination. On the north and south walls are Victorian panels containing bright mosaic depictions of saints and angels, and just inside the entrance on the east wall is a very large monument, executed in high relief, to the founder of the Hospital by John Bacon (1779). This was considered by Sir Nikolaus Pevsner to be 'one of the noblest and most sensitive of its date in England'.

ST GEORGE THE MARTYR, SOUTHWARK
Borough High Street at Long Lane, SE1
(John Price, 1734-6)

There was a church here in 1122 which belonged to the Abbey of Bermondsey. It was rebuilt in the fourteenth century, and repaired and enlarged in 1629. In medieval times, travellers passed through Southwark on their way to the Continent, and it was at the Church of St George that Henry V broke his journey on 26 April 1417 to offer prayers before continuing on his way. According to the seventeenth-century chronicler, Anthony Wood, it was from here, in 1658, that Oliver Cromwell's body was escorted to Somerset House for its lying-in-state. By the early eighteenth century St George's was in poor repair, and in 1732 the parish was granted £6,000 by the Fifty New Churches Commission towards the cost of rebuilding. John Price was appointed to make the designs, and work on the new church started in 1734.

◆

St George the Martyr, Southwark

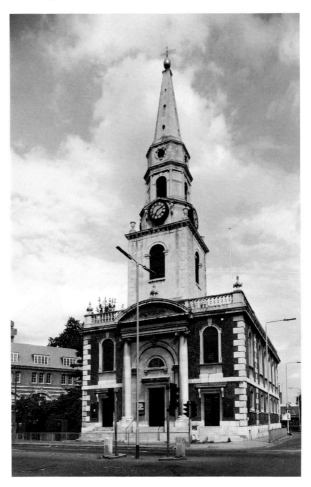

St George's, a handsome red brick building, embellished with white stone, is well placed on an island site. The square stone tower has diminishing octagonal upper stages crowned by a spire. The interior is characteristic of the eighteenth century with an open chancel and sanctuary, galleries and low box pews. The flat ceiling, adorned with cherubs half hidden by clouds, is the work of Basil Champneys in 1897 and was repaired in a general restoration of 1951 carried out by T. F. Ford. The Stuart Royal Arms came from St Michael's, Wood Street, and there is a very fine free-standing pulpit, supported on four Ionic columns.

Bishop Bonner, imprisoned in the Marshalsea by Elizabeth I, was buried in the churchyard in 1569, although it is not certain whether his remains still lie there. Charles Dickens, who knew the Marshalsea well, made it the birthplace of his heroine Little Dorrit. St George's vestry in which she found shelter in childhood and where she later married, is known as 'Little Dorrit Vestry'. She is depicted in a panel of the new east window designed by Marion Grant in the post-war restoration.

ST GILES'S, CAMBERWELL
Camberwell Church Street, SE5
(George Gilbert Scott and
William B. Moffatt, 1842-4)

The foundation of St Giles's, Camberwell is ancient, and is one of the few London churches listed in Domesday Book. From 1152 until the Dissolution of the Monasteries it belonged to Bermondsey Abbey by which it was entirely rebuilt in about 1500. With later additions and restorations it survived until 1841 when, to the consternation of the parish, it was totally devastated by fire. A competition held to select a design for a new church was won by George Gilbert Scott and his partner, William B. Moffatt. In later life, Scott recalled: 'the pains which I took over this church were only equalled by the terror with which I attended the meetings of the committee.' He went on to add that the incumbent 'was determined to have a good church, and so far as his day permitted, he got it'. The *Ecclesiologist* agreed, pronouncing it 'one of the finest ecclesiastical structures of modern days'.

The church is a large cruciform building with a central steeple, in the late thirteenth-century style, correct in its detail, and built in stone. This was an expensive after-thought occasioned by Scott's conversion to the exclusive use of real material while the work was in progress. However, the fittings do not match the purity of the architecture, the seats having been made with Mr Pratt's patent carving machine. The original galleries have since been removed and the interior, for once, actually improved by a coat of whitewash applied by Sir Ninian Comper after the Second World War, when he also coloured the reredos. The glass in the east window, inspired by Ruskin's study of thirteenth-century glass at Chartres and executed by Ward and Nixon, is the outstanding feature of the interior. The sedilia and piscina from the old church have been replaced in the chancel, and on a panel under the south transept window is a set of brasses dating from 1492 to 1637. The gargoyles on the south-west turret include a likeness of W. E. Gladstone despite protests by the Tory vicar that so obstreperous a Liberal was unfit to be commemorated on a sacred building.

LEFT St Giles's, Camberwell

RIGHT St Mary Magdalene, Bermondsey

ST MARY MAGDALENE, BERMONDSEY
Bermondsey Street, SE1 (1675-7)

St Mary Magdalene's, built beside the Cluniac Priory of St Saviour for their 'servants and tenants', is first mentioned in 1296, and was made parochial at the time of the Dissolution of the Monasteries. A subsequent building became ruinous and was pulled down in the early 1670s to make way for the present church. The architect is not known but the builder was Charley Stanton, who incorporated into the Wren-like building two thirteenth-century arches from the original church. In 1830 a number of repairs were carried out by George Porter, a local man, who gave St Mary's its endearing Gothic turrets and embattled west front. The divergent styles are brought together under a covering of beige stucco.

The seventeenth-century interior survives with the addition of galleries and an extended chancel. An entablature supported on Tuscan columns is broken to create a crossing, above which the groined ceiling of the nave is made cruciform. The old furnishings include an interesting square churchwardens' pew with seating all round and a four-sided reading desk, the reredos which was reconstructed from the original in 1907, and two fine early chandeliers of the Dutch type. A Puritan rector once delivered himself of a sermon here which ran to 69 pages, finishing with 'one hundred and twenty-seventhly'. In 1611 another Puritan rector cut down and burned the Parish maypole. The Costermongers' Harvest Festival is held here in September; it is often attended by the Pearly Kings and Queens.

The parishes of St Olave's, St John's, Horsleydown and St Luke's are united with that of St Mary Magdalene's which stands in a large garden with trees, seats and rosebeds.

ST MARY'S, ROTHERHITHE
St Marychurch Street, SE16
(1714-15; Tower, Launcelot Dowbiggin, 1739)

Even today there is a village atmosphere about this riverside church. A place of worship has stood here since the thirteenth century when it belonged to the Abbey of Bermondsey, but only the foundations of the tower and a few stones in the west wall above the organ gallery survive from that time. The old church lay lower than the present one and was constantly being flooded. As a result the structure was so weakened by the beginning of the eighteenth century that the parishioners petitioned for a new church from the Commissioners of the Fifty New Churches Act of 1711. Despite the poignant wording of their request, it was turned down and they were instructed to raise the money for themselves. This was not easy and although work started on the new church in 1714, the project took many years to complete.

It is an unostentatious little building of yellow brick with rubbed red brick and stone trimmings. The tower, also of brick and stone, is finished by a pretty little stone steeple, showing a circle of freestanding columns topped by an obelisk. The interior displays a barrel ceiling supported by four enormous plaster pillars containing hearts of oak taken from the masts of ships. The altar in the Epiphany Chapel and two bishop's chairs, one in the north aisle and one in the apse, are constructed from timber taken from the 'Fighting Temeraire', a vessel which played a notable part in the Battle of Trafalgar. The reredos contains some fine original carving. Opposite to it, on the west wall, is the organ, an exceptionally fine 3-manual by the second John Byfield dating from 1764. It rests on an attractive gallery supported by exceedingly slender cast-iron posts with gilded capitals. A magnificent monument commemorates John Wade, 'King's Carver in his Majesty's Yards at Deptford and Woolwich', who died in 1743. Another touching memorial of 1784 commemorates Prince Lee Boo, whose father (a reputed cannibal) had befriended the crew of the East Indiaman 'Antelope' when it foundered on his remote Pacific island. In gratitude, the prince was invited to England to see the sights, but on arrival caught smallpox and died aged twenty. He is buried in the churchyard.

RIGHT St Mary's, Rotherhithe

ST PETER'S, WALWORTH
Liverpool Grove, SE17
(Sir John Soane, 1823-5)

St Peter's, paid for in part by the so-called Water-loo Commission, was the first of Sir John Soane's three London churches, each of which resembles the other two, St Peter's bearing a particular likeness to Holy Trinity, Marylebone. It is rectangular, built in yellow stock brick with tall, round-headed windows on both sides. On the west front a stretched tower, crowned with an attenuated pepperpot, rises centrally behind a balustrade carried on four huge, recessed Ionic columns forming a portico. The interior is elegant but austere, with flat ceilings and galleries on Doric pillars. Above the galleries rise rounded arches on

St Peter's, Walworth

thin octagonal columns. The chancel, its limits defined by a graceful, wide arch at either end, is unaltered and contains the original Grecian altar-piece painted in imitation of Siena marble. A remarkable feature of the church is the undercroft, although this is rarely open.

St Peter's was damaged during the Second World War, but has been sympathetically restored.

◆

Also in Southwark is the Church of the Most Holy Trinity, Dockhead (1951–60) by that underrated architect, H. S. Goodhart-Rendel.

◆

WANDSWORTH

◆

ALL SAINTS, TOOTING GRAVENEY
Franciscan Road, SW17
(Temple Moore, 1904-06)

Tooting derives from the Manor of Tooting and Streatham which stood in this area in Norman times, and Graveney refers to the Gravenell family which held the manor in the twelfth and thirteenth centuries.

All Saints was built to designs by Temple Moore with money bequeathed by Lady Augusta Brudenell-Bruce in memory of her husband, who died in 1897. It is large and noble, constructed in yellow stock brick in the style of the fourteenth century. The south-west battlemented tower is flanked on either side by belfry windows, and beyond the chancel is a square-ended Lady Chapel.

The interior is unexpectedly attractive and of beautiful proportions, having seven bays with double aisles to the naves, single to the chancel. The vault is of timber, painted white. Most of the furnishings are Italian and French, collected by Canon Stephens, the first vicar, and adapted by

Sir Walter Tapper. The principal treasure is a Baroque reredos from Bologna, finely carved and gilded. Above this is a copy of Velasquez's painting, 'The Crucifixion'. The very large wooden candlesticks, ten feet high, came from Florence, and there is an ancient iron grille from a church near Lake Como. The stained glass in the east window is by Victor Milner, and the fine Harrison organ is housed in a gilded case designed by Sir Walter Tapper.

◆

ALL SAINTS, WANDSWORTH
Wandsworth High Street, SW18 (1779)

All Saints, founded in the twelfth or thirteenth century, was the parish church of Wandsworth village, one of five medieval villages now comprising the urban district of Wandsworth. It was rebuilt in 1630, and subsquently repaired and altered several times. By 1779, however, it was in such bad order that it had again to be rebuilt except for the 1630 tower and the 1724 north aisle. There followed substantial alterations in 1841 when the tower was refaced and raised; and in the

All Saints, Tooting Graveney

ABOVE All Saints, Wandsworth

LEFT St Mary's, Battersea

1890s a large chancel was added. Part of the tower was destroyed by a bomb in 1941, but was repaired in a post-war restoration, completed in 1955.

The exterior, in brick, is quite plain with a square tower and round-headed windows. A simple Tuscan porch forms the entrance to the south side of the church. Inside it is tunnel-vaulted on Doric columns of wood, painted to look like marble, with a frieze and cornice. The galleries lie back from the aisles and are approached by a fine staircase. There is a churchwardens' square pew still surviving, and the small marble font and pulpit on a baluster shaft are original. Monuments include a damaged brass of 1420 to Nicholas Maudyt, and memorials to Henry Smith (1627) and Susanna Powell (1630) showing them kneeling under arches – the corbels on which they rest are formed of jawless skulls.

ST ANNE'S, WANDSWORTH
St Ann's Hill, SW18
(Robert Smirke, 1820-22)

St Anne's, designed by Robert Smirke as a chapel of ease for part of the rapidly developing parish of Wandsworth, was built on a hill-top site in what was then open country to the east of the river Wandle. It was the fifth of the churches paid for by the 1818 Commission, and it was made parochial in 1850.

The body of the church is in brick with an Ionic stone portico to the front. The tower, which rises above the portico, is extremely tall, circular and with a domed cap so suggestive in shape that it has often been called 'The Pepper Pot Church'. St Anne's was slightly damaged in the Second World War, but has since been well restored. The interior is open and spacious, well lit by clear glass windows. An amusing episode in its history concerns a dispute in 1822 between the vestry and the Bishop of Winchester in whose diocese St Anne's was included. Half the vestry wanted the churchyard fence to be constructed in iron, the other half in oak; at length they agreed on a compromise: the fence should be built of both materials. The Bishop objected, and was so incensed when they

ignored his injunction that he refused to consecrate the ground, and to this day there have been no burials in the graveyard.

◆

ST MARY'S, BATTERSEA
Battersea Church Road, SW11
(Joseph Dixon, 1775-7)

The church which stood here at the time of the Conquest was granted to Westminster Abbey in 1067. Because of this connection workmen from the Abbey were frequently employed at the Battersea site, and the great fourteenth-century master mason, Henry Yevele, built an eastern gable to the church containing a window, the shape of which is retained in the present building. The medieval church lingered on into the 1770s, too small and too decrepit for the fashionable suburb that had grown up around it, so a competition was held to choose an architect to design a new building. It was won by Joseph Dixon, the churchwarden, whose simple village church followed the ground plan of the old structure.

St Mary's stands on its riverside site, looking much the same as when it was built. It is a modest rectangle in dark brick trimmed in stone, with a square tower and copper spire rising centrally behind a wide, white portico. The eighteenth-century interior is unexceptional, although the brackets supporting the front of the galleries are unusual, having benefactions inscribed upon them. The 1631 stained glass in the east window gleams yellow and gold; on either side are circular transparencies of the Dove and the Lamb by James Pearson (1796). Among the splendid monuments is one to Henry St John, Viscount Bolingbroke (died 1751) and his second wife with epitaphs written by himself. A wall cartouche with shields, cherubs' heads, flowers and fruit commemorates Sir John Fleet, Lord Major of the City in 1693 (died 1712), and a memorial to Sir Edward Wynter (died 1686) records:

Alone unarmed a Tigre he opprest
And crushed to death ye monster of a Beast.
Thrice-twenty mounted Moors he overthrew
Single on foot, some wounded, some he slew
Dispers'd ye rest; what more could Samson do!

LEFT St Anne's, Wandsworth

RIGHT St Mary's, Putney

In St Mary's in 1631, Edward Hyde, later Earl of Clarendon, married his first wife; and here, in 1782, William Blake married the daughter of a Battersea market gardener. She, being unable to write, signed the marriage certificate with an 'X'.

◆

ST MARY'S, PUTNEY
Putney High Street, SW15
(Edward Lapidge, 1836)

St Mary's was originally a chapel of ease to Wimbledon. It was rebuilt in the fifteenth century and again in 1836 by Edward Lapidge, who retained the old tower and a tiny fan-vaulted chantry chapel which had been added in the early sixteenth century by the Bishop of Ely, who was a native of Putney. The church was devastated by fire in 1977, but fortunately the chantry survived. The rest was rebuilt by Ronald Sims and the furnishings rearranged to face an altar under the north arcade. The old church was the scene of a

Cromwellian meeting in 1647. It is said that Generals Fairfax and Ireton sat round the Communion Table defiantly wearing their hats.

◆

ST NICHOLAS'S, TOOTING GRAVENEY
Church Lane, SW17
(T. W. Atkinson, 1832-3)

A place of worship at Tooting Graveney is mentioned in Domesday Book. The Saxon church was an eccentric little building of such charm that there was a public outcry at its proposed demolition : the *Gentlemen's Magazine* of August 1831 carried a passionate declamation against the scheme, but the vestry had its way and the new Gothic church of St Nicholas was erected a little to the west of the old church, which was afterwards demolished.

The present church is of stock brick with a pinnacled tower and some fancy Decorated tracery. The modern glass in the windows of the apse is by A. L. Wilkinson (1954), and there are some early monuments including the funeral achievements of Sir James Bateman, Lord Mayor of London.

◆

LEFT St Nicholas's, Tooting Graveney

SELECT BIBLIOGRAPHY

◆

BETJEMAN, John, *The City of London Churches*, Pitkin Pictorials, 1974

BETJEMAN, John, with CLARKE, Basil, *English Churches*, Vista Books, 1964

BLATCH, Mervyn, *A Guide to London's Churches*, Constable, 1978

BUMPUS, T. F., *Ancient London Churches* (2 vols), T. Werner Laurie, 1908

CLARKE, Basil F. L., *Parish Churches of London*, Batsford, 1966

COBB, Gerald, *The Old Churches of London*, Batsford, 1948

COBB, Gerald, *City of London Churches*, Batsford, 1977

COLVIN, Howard, *A Biographical Dictionary of British Architects, 1600–1840*, John Murray, 1978

CROSS, F. L. (ed.), *The Oxford Dictionary of the Christian Church*, Oxford University Press, 1957

NAIRN, Ian, *Nairn's London*, Penguin Books, 1966

PEVSNER, Nikolaus, *London: The Cities of London and Westminster*, Penguin Books, revised edition by Bridget Cherry, 1962

PEVSNER, Nikolaus, *London Except the Cities of London and Westminster*, Penguin Books, 1952

STAMP, Gavin, and AMERY, Colin, *Victorian Buildings of London, 1837–87*, Architectural Press, 1980

STOW, John (ed. KINGSFORD, C. L.), *Survey of London*, Oxford University Press, 1908

SUMMERSON, John, *Architecture in Britain 1530–1830*, Pelican History of Art, Penguin Books, 1970

SUMMERSON, John, *Georgian London*, Pleiades, 1945

The Survey of London, Athlone Press, 43 volumes to date

WEINREB, Ben, and HIBBERT, Christopher (eds), *The London Encyclopaedia*, Macmillan, new edition 1987

YOUNG, Elizabeth and Wayland, *Old London Churches*, Faber & Faber, 1968

YOUNG, Elizabeth and Wayland, *London Churches*, Grafton Books, 1986

◆

INDEX

◆

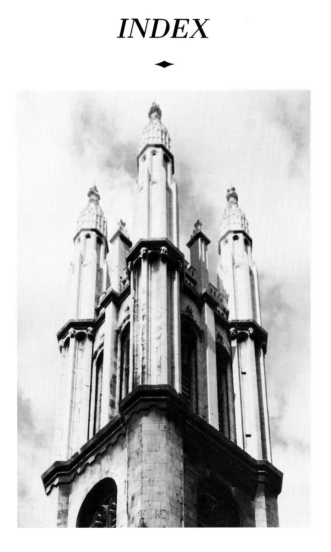

POSTCODE INDEX